600 YEARS
OF
BRISTOL POETRY

EDITED BY EDWARD MARTIN
AND BILL PICKARD

Arts and Leisure Committee
of the City and County of Bristol
1973

First published 1973 by
The Arts & Leisure Committee
of the City and County of Bristol

ISBN 0 9502 807 04

P & S Dept. W246

FOREWORD

In 1973 Bristol celebrates the 600th anniversary of the granting of its charter as a county by King Edward III. The celebrations are to take many forms but it was a most happy inspiration and one that made a ready appeal to the Arts and Leisure Committee of the City Council that the occasion should also be marked by the publication of this volume of Bristol poetry, and I warmly commend the book to my fellow citizens. Over the centuries Bristol has produced poets and poems of distinction and it is a matter of pride and pleasure that a city such as ours, rich in history and with a great heritage of the past, should find satisfaction in its own creative literature.

I would pay tribute to the work of the editors, Mr. Edward Martin, Senior English Master of the Cathedral School and two helpers from his sixth form Sebastian Rahtz and Simon Littlewood and Mr. Bill Pickard, Director of Literature of the Arts Centre who have undertaken the difficult task of research and selection. Thanks are also due to Mr. Charles Hobday for the original suggestion for the publication of this book.

The Committee are also grateful to Councillor Mrs. Yvonne Craig, Chairman of the Libraries Visiting Sub-Committee and to Mr. W. S. Haugh, City Librarian, for their interest and enthusiasm.

R. E. Morris, *Councillor*

Chairman of the Arts and Leisure Committee
Bristol City Council

ACKNOWLEDGEMENTS

AS I WALKED OUT ONE EVENING: W. H. Auden: Collected Shorter Poems 1927–1957: *Faber & Faber, Ltd.*

BRISTOL AND CLIFTON: Sir John Betjeman: Collected Poems.
BRISTOL: *John Murray (Publishers) Ltd.*

BALLAD OF THE FIVE CONTINENTS (Union Street): Charles Causley
CRISTO DE BRISTOL (Johnny Alleluia): *Rupert Hart-Davis.*

THE PHOENIX-HEARTED, THE COMING OF APRIL, LOWER THAN THE ANGELS, STAR-FISHER: Iris Murdoch: *Poet Venturers, Bristol* 1938.

NEWFOUNDLAND STREET: Richard Ball: Avalon 3: *Outposts Publications.*

AT THE SCENE OF THE ACCIDENT — BRISTOL: Bill Pickard: *Harlech Television.*

CLIFTON—A LAMENT FOR THE TRAMS: Gerard Irvine: Sunset & Evening Star: *The Fortune Press.*

CLERKSHIP: Stuart Hoskins: Farewell to Severn Shore: *Outposts Publications.*

SEA WALLS, OCTOBER 1944: N. H. Langran: *Unicorn* 1960.

THE BRISTOL UNICORNS: Maurice Carpenter: *Unicorn* 1960.

SONG TO A MYTHICAL BEAST: Norman Harvey: *Unicorn* 1960.

AN EARLY PARACHUTE DESCENT IN BRISTOL: W. E. Heasell: *Unicorn* 1960.

WITHIN THE CITY LIMITS: Alan Crang: *The Circle In The Square.*

THE DUTCH HOUSF: Andrea Hopkins: *The Circle In The Square.*

THE DOWNS: Jill Racy: *The Circle In The Square.*

EARLY DAYS: Freda Bromhead: *The Circle In The Square.*

SLUM CLEARANCE: M. C. Beeching: *Poems From Bristol Schools* 1965.

ORDER: John Clee: Blue Feather Poems: *The Burleigh Press.*

SUMMER IN CLIFTON: Donald Hughes: Love and Laughter: *Rankin Brothers Ltd.*

TEMPLE CHURCH (as THF TEMPLE): Abe Adams: In Perspective.

CHATTERTON: C. H. Hobday: *Bristol EVENING POST.*

BRISTOL THEMES: Ray Webber: *Bristol EVENING POST.*

REFLECTIONS OF BRISTOL: Elizabeth Maggs: *Bristol EVENING POST.*

BRISTOL—AN EXILE'S VIEW: Dave Sampson: *Bristol EVENING POST.*

Author	*Contents*	*Page*
MICHAEL DRAYTON	Poly-Olbion: The Third Song	1
JOHN EVELYN	Diary: In Bath And Bristol	2
SAMUEL PEPYS	Diary: And So To Bristol	2
ALEXANDER POPE	Letters To Martha Blount	3
RICHARD SAVAGE	London And Bristol Compared	5
WILLIAM GOLDWIN	A Poetical Description Of Bristol	7
ANON	An Attack On The New Theatre 1766	9
WILLIAM HEARD	A Sentimental Journey	10
ANN YEARSLEY	Clifton Hill	12
MARIA EDGEWORTH	Letter To Mr Ruxton	12
THOMAS HOBHOUSE	Kingsweston Hill	13
THOMAS CHATTERTON	Mynstrelles Songe (from Aella)	14
	Stay Curyous Traveller	15
	Elegy I	16
	Clifton	17
	Betsy Of The Hill	18
JOSEPH COTTLE	Epitaph For Proposed Monument To Chatterton	18
ROMAINE JOSEPH THORN	Bristolia	19
ROBERT LOVELL	Bristol: A Satire	20
ROBERT SOUTHEY	The Ebb Tide	23
	To A Goose	23
	Sonnet VI	24
S. T. COLERIDGE	Lines On Brockley Coombe	24
WILLIAM WORDSWORTH	Tintern Abbey	25
WILLIAM MORGAN	Long Ashton	29
T. L. BEDDOES	Dream-Pedlary	32
	The Ghosts' Moonshine	33
	Dirge	34
	Song: How Many Times Do I Love Thee	34
CHARLES ELTON	Sonnet On St. Mary Redcliff	35
W. S. LANDOR	To The River Avon	35
JOHN JAMES	Avon River	36
STANLEY HUTTON	On R. H. Barham	37
FRANCIS BARHAM	Bristowa's Prophecy	38
THE MAN IN THE SUN	Bristol Beauties	40
J. A. SYMONDS	Clifton And A Lad's Love	42
WILLIAM C. POCOCK	Durdham Downs	44
T. E. BROWN	Clifton	45
	Fives' Court	45
M. C. TYNDALL	Bristol Bells	46
ROSE SHARLAND	The Bells Of Abbot's Leigh	47
A. L. SALMON	In The Dim City—Bristol	48

Author	*Contents*	*Page*
IRIS MURDOCH	The Phoenix-Hearted	49
(aged 18)	The Coming Of April	49
	Star-Fisher	50
	Lower Than The Angels	51
A. L. SALMON	By Severn's Banks	51
W. H. AUDEN	As I Walked Out One Evening	52
JOHN BETJEMAN	Bristol And Clifton	54
	Bristol	56
CLAIRE HALL	The Hole In The Wall	57
RICHARD BALL	Newfoundland Street	58
	Bathurst Wharf	59
BILL PICKARD	At The Scene Of The Accident—Bristol	60
	Stoke House 1669	61
GERARD IRVINE	Clifton—A Lament For The Trams	62
W. L. BOWLES	Bristol	63
STUART HOSKINS	Clerkship	64
N. H. LANGRAN	Sea Walls, October 1944	65
CHARLES CAUSLEY	Ballad Of The Five Continents	66
	Cristo De Bristol	67
ABE ADAMS	Temple Church	68
ALAN CRANG	Within The City Limits	69
ROBERT GORDON	Voyage 47	70
MAURICE CARPENTER	The Bristol Unicorns	72
NORMAN HARVEY	Song To A Mythical Beast	73
FREDA BROMHEAD	Early Days	74
	Clifton Morning	75
MARIAN LIEBMANN	Bristol, City Of Sadness	76
	Double Yellows	76
DIANA HENDRY	City Skin	77
W. S. LANDOR	Clifton	77
M. C. BEECHING	Slum Clearance	78
C. H. HOBDAY	A Roman Tombstone	80
	Chatterton	80
JOHN CLEE	Order	81
DONALD HUGHES	Summer In Clifton	81
ROBIN LLOYD	Bristol Fashion	82
	Genius Ahoy!	83
ANDREA HOPKINS	The Dutch House	83
JILL RACY	The Old Graveyard, Clifton	84
	The Downs	85
WILLIAM E. HEASELL	An Early Parachute Descent In Bristol	85
ANON	Limerick	85
RAY WEBBER	Bristol Themes	86
ELIZABETH MAGGS	Reflections Of Bristol	87
DAVE SAMPSON	Bristol—An Exile's View	88

(From)

POLY-OLBION
THE THIRD SONG

Then came the lusty *Froome*, the first of Floods that met
Fair *Avon* ent'ring into fruitful *Somerset*,
With her attending Brooks; and her to *Bath* doth bring,
Much honoured by that place, *Minerva's* sacred Spring.
To noble *Avon*, next, clear *Chute* as kindly came,
To *Bristow* her to bear, the fairest seat of Fame:
To entertain this Flood, as great a mind that hath,
And striving in that kind far to excel the *Bath*.
As when some wealthy lord prepares to entertain
A man of high account, and feast his gallant train,
Of him that did the like, doth seriously enquire
His diet, his device, his service, his attire;
That varying everything (exampled by his store)
He every way may pass what th' other did before:
Even so this City doth; the prospect of which place
To her fair building adds an admirable grace;
Well-fashion'd as the best, and with a double wall,
As brave as any town; but yet excelling all
For easement, that to health is requisite and meet;
Her piled shores, to keep her delicate and sweet:
Hereto, she hath her tides; that when she is opprest
With heat or drought, still pour their floods upon her breast.

To *Mendip* then the Muse upon the South inclines,
Which is the only store, and coffer of her mines:
Elsewhere the fields and meads their sundry traffics suit:
The forests yield her wood, the orchards give her fruit.

As in some rich man's house his several charges lie,
There stands his wardrobe, here remains his treasury;
His large provision there, of fish, of fowl, and neat;
His cellars for his wines, his larders for his meat;
There banquet-houses, walks for pleasure; here again
Cribs, graners, stables, barns, the other to maintain:
So this rich country hath, itself what may suffice;
Or that which through exchange a smaller want supplies.

MICHAEL DRAYTON 1622

IN BATH AND BRISTOL

The *Faciate* of this Cathedrall is remarkable for the Historical Carving: The *Kings Bath* is esteemed the fairest in *Europe*; The Towne is intirely built of stone, but the streetes narrow, uneven & unpleasant: Here we trifled & bath'd, & intervisited with the company who frequent the place, for health &c: till 30th & then went to *Bristoll* a Citty emulating *London*, not for its large extent, but manner of building, shops, bridge: Traffique: Exchange, Marketplace &c. The Governor shew'd us the Castle, of no great concernment: The City wholy Mercantile, as standing neere the famous *Severne*, commodiously for *Ireland* & the Western world: Here I first saw the manner of refining Suggar, & casting it into loaves, where we had collation of Eggs fried in the suggar furnace, together with excellent Spanish Wine; but what was most stupendious to me, was the rock of St. *Vincent*, a little distance from the Towne, the precipice whereoff is equal to any thing of that nature I have seene in the most confragose cataracts of the *Alpes:* The river gliding betwene them after an extraordinary depth: Here we went searching for *Diamonds*, & to the hot Well of Water at its foote: There is also on the side of this horrid Alp, a very romantic seate. & so we returned that Evening to *Bathe*.

JOHN EVELYN — July 1654

'AND SO TO BRISTOL'

The way bad, but country good, about two o'clock, where set down at the Horseshoe, and there, being trimmed by a very handsome fellow, 2*s*., walked with my wife and people through the city, which is in every respect another London, that one can hardly know it, to stand in the country, no more than that. No carts, it standing generally on vaults, only dog-carts. So to the Three Crowns Tavern I was directed; but, when I come in, the master told me that he had newly given over the selling of wine; it seems, grown rich; and so went to the Sun; and there Deb. going with W. Hewer and Betty Turner to see her uncle [Butts], and leaving my wife with the mistress of the house, I to see the quay, which is a most large and noble place; and to see the new ship building by Bally, neither he nor Furzer being in town. It will be a fine ship. Spoke with the foreman, and did give the boys that kept the cabin 2*s*.

Walked back to the Sun, where I find Deb. come back, and with her, her uncle, a sober merchant, very good company, and so like one of our sober, wealthy, London merchants, as pleased me mightily. Here we dined, and much good talk with him, *7s. 6d.:* a messenger to Sir John Knight, who was not at home, *6d.* Then walked with him [Butts] and my wife and company round the quay, and to the ship; and he shewed me the Custom-house, and made me understand many things of the place, and led us through Marsh Street, where our girl was born. But, Lord! the joy that was among the old poor people of the place, to see Mrs. Willet's daughter, it seems her mother being a brave woman and mightily beloved! And so brought us a back way by surprize to his house, where a substantial good house, and well furnished; and did give us good entertainment of strawberries, a whole venison-pasty, cold, and plenty of brave wine, and above all Bristoll milk.

SAM PEPYS June 13, 1668

TO MARTHA BLOUNT

Bristol, Munday.

I hardly knew what I undertook when I said I would give you some Account of this place. Nothing can do it but a Picture, it is so unlike any Scene you ever saw. But I'll begin at least, & reserve the rest to my next letter. From Bath you go along the River, or its Side, the Road lying generally in sight of it, on each Bank are steep rising Hills cloathd with Wood at top, and sloping toward the stream in Green Meadows, intermixt with white Houses, Mills & Bridges, this for 7 & 8 miles, then you come in sight of Bristol, the River winding at the bottom of steeper banks to the Town where you see twenty odd Pyramids smoking over the Town (which are Glasshouses) and a vast Extent of Houses red & white. You come first to Old Walls, & over a Bridge built on both sides like London bridge, and as much crowded, with a strange mixture of Seamen, women, children, loaded Horses, Asses, & Sledges with Goods dragging along, all together, without posts to separate them. From thence you come to a Key along the old Wall with houses on both sides, and in the middle of the street, as far as you can see, hundreds of Ships, their Masts as thick as they can stand by one another, which is the oddest & most surprising sight imaginable. This street is fuller of them, than the Thames from London Bridge to Deptford, & at certain times only, the Water rises to carry them out; so that at other times, a Long Street full of ships in the Middle & Houses on both sides looks like a Dream. Passing still along by the River you come to a Rocky way on one Side, overlooking green Hills on the other; On that rocky way rise several white Houses, and over them red rocks, and as you go further, more Rocks above rocks, mixd with green bushes, and of different colour stone. This at a Mile's end, terminates in the House of the Hot well, whereabouts lye several pretty Lodging Houses open to the River with Walks of Trees. When you have seen the Hills seem to shut upon you & to stop any further way, you go into the House & looking out of the Back door, a vast Rock of 100 foot high, of red, white, green, blue & yellowish Marbles, all blotch'd & variegated strikes you quite in the face, & turning on the left, there opens the River at a vast depth below, winding in & out, & accompanied on both sides with a Continued Range of Rocks up to the Clouds, of a hundred Colours, one behind another, & so to the end of the Prospect quite to the Sea. But the Sea nor the Severn you do not see, the Rocks & River fill the Eye, and terminate the View, much like the broken Scenes behind one another in a Playhouse. From the room where I write, I see the Tyde rising, and filling all the bottom between these Scenes of Rocks, on the Sides of which on one hand are Buildings, some white, some red, every where up & down like the steepest side of Richmond to the Thames, mixd with Trees & Shrubs, but much wilder, and huge Shaggy Marbles, some in Points, some in Caverns, hanging all over & under them in a thousand shapes.

ALEXANDER POPE 19 November, 1739

Upon the top of those high Rocks by the Hotwell, which I've described to you, there runs on One side a large Down, of fine Turf, for about three miles. It looks too frightful to approach the brink, & look down upon the River; but in many parts of this Down the Vallyes descend gently, & you see all along the Windings of the Stream, & the Opening of the Rocks, which turn, & close in upon you, from space to space, for several Miles, on toward the Sea. There is first near Bristol a little Village upon this Down, called Clifton, where are very pretty Lodginghouses overlooking all the woody hills, & steep cliffs, & very green Vallies: within half a mile of the wells; where in the Summer it must be delicious walking & riding, for the Plain extends one way many miles. Particularly there is a Tower, that stands close at the Edge of the highest Rock, & sees the Stream turn quite round it; & All the Banks one way are Wooded, in a gentle slope for near a mile high quite green; the other bank all inaccessible rock, of a hundred colours & odd shapes, some hundred foot perpendicular. I am told that one may ride ten miles further on an Even Turf, on a Ridge, that on one side views the River Severn & the banks steeper & steeper quite to the Open Sea, & on the other side a vast Woody Vale as far as the Eye can stretch; & all before you the Opposite Coast of Wales beyond the Severn again. But this I have not been able to see; nor would one, but in better weather: when one may dine or lye there, or cross a narrow part of the Stream to the nearest Point in Wales, where Mr Allen & Mr Hook last Summer lay some Nights in the cleanest & best Cottage in the World with excellent Provisions, under a Hill on the Margin of the Severne. Let him describe it to You, & pray tell him we are much in fear for his health, not having had a line since he left us.

The City of Bristol itself is very unpleasant, & no civilized Company in it. Only the Collector of the Customs would have brought me acquainted with Merchants, of whom I hear no great Character. The streets are as crowded as London but the best Image I can give you of it is, Tis as if Wapping and Southwark were ten-times as big, or all their people run into London. Nothing is fine in it but the Square, which is larger than Grosvenor-Square, & wellbuilded, with a very fine brass Statue in the middle, of K. William on Horseback: And the Key, which is full of Ships & goes round half this Square. The College Green is pretty & (like the Square) set with Trees, with a very fine Old Cross of Gothic curious work in the middle, but spoild with the folly of new gilding it, that takes away all the Venerable Antiquity. There is a Cathedral very neat, & 19 Parish Churches.

ALEXANDER POPE 24 November, 1739

(From)

LONDON AND BRISTOL COMPAR'D
A SATIRE

Two Sea-port Cities mark *Britannia's* Fame,
And these from Commerce different Honours claim.
What different Honours shall the Muses pay,
While one inspires and one untunes the Lay?
Now silver *Isis* bright'ning flows along,
Echoing from *Oxford's* Shore each classic Song;
Then weds with *Tame;* and these, O *London,* see
Swelling with naval Pride, the Pride of Thee!
Wide deep unsullied *Thames* meand'ring glides
And bears thy Wealth on mild majestic Tides.
Thy Ships, with gilded Palaces that vie,
In glitt'ring Pomp, strike wond'ring *China*'s Eye;
And thence returning bear, in splendid State,
To *Britain*'s Merchants, *India*'s eastern Freight.
India, her Treasures from her western Shores,
Due at thy Feet, a willing Tribute pours;
Thy warring Navies distant Nations awe,
And bid the World obey thy righteous Law.
Thus shine thy manly Sons of lib'ral Mind;

Thy Change deep-busied, yet as Courts refin'd;
Councils, like Senates that enforce Debate
With fluent Eloquence, and Reason's Weight.
Whose Patriot Virtue, lawless Pow'r controuls;
Their *British* emulating *Roman* Souls.
Of these the worthiest still selected stand,
Still lead the Senate, and still save the Land:
Social, not selfish, here, O Learning trace
Thy Friends, the Lovers of all human Race!
In a dark Bottom sunk, O *Bristol* now,
With native Malice, lift thy low'ring Brow!
Then as some Hell-born Sprite, in mortal Guise,
Borrows the Shape of Goodness and belies,
All fair, all smug to yon proud Hall invite,
To feast all Strangers ape an Air Polite!
From *Cambria* drain'd, or *England*'s western Coast,
Not elegant yet costly Banquets boast!
Revere, or seem the Stranger to revere;
Praise, fawn, profess, be all Things but sincere;
Insidious now, our bosom Secrets steal,
And these with sly sarcastic Sneer reveal.
Present we meet thy sneaking treach'rous Smiles;
The harmless Absent still thy Sneer reviles;
Such as in Thee all Parts superior find;
The Sneer that marks the Fool and Knave combin'd.
When melting Pity wou'd afford Relief,
The ruthless Sneer that Insult adds to Grief.
What Friendship can'st thou boast? what Honours claim?
To Thee each Stranger owes an injur'd Name.
What Smiles thy Sons must in their Foes excite?
Thy Sons to whom all Discord is Delight;
From whom eternal mutual Railing flows;
Who in each other's Crimes, their own expose;
Thy Sons, though crafty, deaf to Wisdom's Call;
Despising all Men and despis'd by all.
Sons, while thy Clifs a ditch-like River laves,
Rude as thy Rocks, and muddy as thy Waves;
Of Thoughts as narrow as of Words immense;
As full of Turbulence as void of Sense:
Proceed, great *Bristol*, in all-righteous Ways,
And let one Justice heighten yet thy Praise;
Still spare the Catamite and swinge the Whore,
And be, whate'er *Gomorrah* was before.

RICHARD SAVAGE (written in Newgate Gaol) 1743

(From)

A POETICAL DESCRIPTION OF BRISTOL

Now leave the distant Views of distant Fields,
A nearer Circle City-Prospect yields.
Here Pyramids of sacred Temples grow,
And spiral Tops to Heav'nly Ruler show;
Whose virtual Presence fills the Domes below.
A comely Form the stately Buildings grace;
An inward Worship suits the outward Face:
A Worship fairly drawn from two Extremes;
The high *Papistick*, or *Genevan* Schemes;
In Reputation, Sense, and Manners, clear,
To nothing, but enormous Vice, severe.
By standard-Rules of Truth and Honour led,
He shines the Clergy's Pattern, Friend, and Head;
Whose well pois'd Cares in equal Ballance go
To serve the Throne above, and that below.

Above the Confines of this Prelate's Seat,
An old Cathedral venerably great,
From rising Ground a bulky Building rears,
And Prints of Time in rugged Aspect bears.
Injurious Time! thy keenest Rage employ,
And gnaw with Envy what you can't destroy;
Whilst inward Worship shews a cleanly Face,
And true Devotion adds a second Grace,
Omnipotent Eternity protects the Place.

Here double Organ, set with tuneful Keys,
Thro' speaking Tubes melodious Anthems plays;
Whilst Choiral Voices from harmonious Throats,
True Consort make and corresponding Notes.
If airy Trebles elevate the Soul,
The mellow *Base* the rising Joys controul.
In middle Vein the soothing *Tenor* runs,
And two Extremes, like Moderator, shuns.
Mean while the vaulted Canopy rebounds
The vocal Airs and instrumental Sounds;
A faint Resemblance of the Saints above,
Whose Hallelujah's echo Peace and Love,

Beneath the Hill, where this Foundation grows,
Frome's muddy Stream in troubled Water flows;
Where intervening Inlets of the Tide,
A lengthen'd Key, and rising Bank divide.

Here active Scenes of naval Labour reign,
And wooden Cradles infant Ships sustain.
Imperfect some by gradual Working grow,
Some finish'd Hulls in large Proportion show:
O'er slippery Frames some Maiden Vessels ply,
In launching sweeps, and *Neptune*'s Favour try;
Pledges entrusted to the boundless Deep,
(Ye Winds and Waves the Darling's Pledges keep)
Wide Ocean's Bosom is a Gulph of Woe,
Where frightful Scenes in ghastly Figures grow:
Yet how the *floating Islands* fearless go!
Till Age, Misfortune, *Gallick* Fraud or Force,
Dissolve the Frame, or interrupt the Course.
So human Bodies sev'ral Stages have,
From the Babe's Cradle, to the old Man's Grave.
Here useful Docks to nice Perfection brought,
With wooden Ribs, and costly Engines wrought.
An inland Port in hollow'd Bosoms keep,
Where new and shatter'd Gallies safely sleep,
Till Time or Tide remand them to the Deep.

A busier Stage employs the noisy *Key*,
Great Bales of Wealth the World's Increase display;
What different Climes, or distant Lands produce,
Virginia's Weed, or *Spain*'s enriching Juice;
(Two constant Friends for chearful Use design'd,)
Here Side by Side in social Order join'd;
Each Tribute lays at Sovereign GEORGE's Feet,
Then mix in Mirth, and Tipplers Joys compleat:
For moist'ning Draughts and parching smoaky Leaf,
Provide and give a mutual kind Relief.

Here Ships, escap'd from Ocean's dreadful Flood,
Find soft Repose in oozy Beds of Mud;
But when th' alternate Motions of the Tide,
In upward Surge, or downward Ebbings glide,
In pompous Bulk the lofty Vessels ride.
Here lay the *Rangers of the Southern Seas*,
That bore a *Jason*, and return'd a Fleece,
A Fleece, adorn'd like Sacrifice of old,
With ornamental Silks, and costly Gold.

WILLIAM GOLDWIN 1751

"It is not denied that some good Sentiments are found in several "theatrical Pieces; but these will not compensate for the false Notions "of Life, the Impurity, Falsehood and Impiety which they contain. "There are very few, it is to be feared, in which the third Commandment "is not violated: And it is not in the least improbable that the Perusal "and Exhibition of them hath contributed greatly to the Prevalence "of that profane Mention, in a trifling Manner, of the awful Name of the "supreme Being, which disgraces this Christian Country." (From Note to Printer.)

Tho' cautious Craft *at first* the PLAYERS guide,
They fling, when fix'd, th' ensnaring Mask aside.
In their own Colours, unabash'd and bare,
They smartly season their dramatic Ware,
To raise the Laugh; regale with sportful Tone
The Taste, corrupt, that tallies with their own;
Their Jests obscene and Ribaldry diffuse,
Deride Religion, and its Friends abuse;
Fire each rude Passion (check'd each useful Care)
T'insult the Modest, and assault the Fair;
Promote Intrigues, and push the bold Design,
To break thro' Laws, both human and divine;
Make all but Trifles, as when Infants play,
And laugh and reason Sin and Shame away;
Ev'n tho' sad Ruin be by Wiles convey'd
To unsuspecting Innocence betray'd.
So *Nile*'s amphibious Crocodiles decoy,
And, softly soothing, Sycophants destroy.
Who see their Trap, with Sequels which it draws,
Its Dupes commis' rate, and commend the Laws.
How will Domestics quit all due Regard!
How the new 'Prentice prove untimely mar'd!
How Rakes in shameless Insolence ally'd,
And Stews and Strumpets roundly multiply'd!
Of Birds unclean how many a hateful Cage!
The Dregs and Rubbish of the baneful Stage!

This faithful Sketch no Gall of Malice brings;
Misrepresenting neither Men nor Things:
But honest Truth, to every Object due,
Must each delineate in its proper Hue.

If Force and Fraud o'erflow, without the STAGE,
If vile Debauches of an iron Age;
How must their ampler Measures be deriv'd
From this old *Satan*'s *Synagogue* reviv'd!

(From)

'BRISTOL THEATRE'

ANON. 1766

(From)

A SENTIMENTAL JOURNEY

So bring the horses; bring the pillion too:
O'er *Durdam Down* delighted let us ride,
And view from SOUTHWELL's Park the prospect wide.
Now on the Tower of *Dundry* let us stand,
And the vast landscape all around command;
Now, o'er the spacious plain of *Shrubby Ley*,
Let us chat chearful, and the view survey;
Pleasing the rides, and fine the country round,
But Oh, sweet *Clifton!* where shall strains be found,
Thy villa's beauties in just glow to paint,
To which the colouring even of POPE were faint:
Yet had he lived that task performed to see,
"How had it blest mankind, and rescued me!"

High on a hill, with beauteous structures spread,
Delightful *Clifton* rears its rural head;
And looks with pleasure on the vales below,
Where towns are planted, and where rivers flow.
Here, full in view, *Bristolia*'s city lies,
O'er which enraptured glance the gladdened eyes,
Viewing the wood-capt hills which rise around,
Chequered with many a hedge-row's verdant bound.

Now see the *Avon* wind his chalky tide,
And, like a serpent, thro' the green vales glide;
While o'er the stream her vessels COMMERCE tows,
Whence well-earned wealth on busy labour flows.
To variegate the prospect, here is viewed,
The heath all barren, and the rocks all rude:
On which, like mountains, stoney craggs appear,
Pregnant with *gems*, and glittering with *spar*,
And different rocks your wondering eyes survey
Romantic foliage, where bold trees display;
Trees that to heaven aloft their summits shoot,
Deep darting through the rocks each fib'rous root.
These views from GOLDNEY's *Terrace* you command,
Work of vast labour, and a skilful hand!
GOLDNEY, whose spirit, all untamed and bold,
And, like the lion's, formed in noblest mold:
No difficulties daunt, no cost deters,
In resolution fixed, he perseveres:

Through iron rocks an hundred fathom down
He pierces, and commands the stream to run,
Obedient upward, forming at his will
The crystaline canal or gurgling rill.

Deep in the rock his coolly *grotto* lies,
Of splendid stones, where brilliant pillars rise;
Where every shell, of every glowing hue,
In elegant composure charm the view:
"Where lingering drops from mineral roofs distil,
"And pointed crystals, break the sparkling rill;
"Unpolished gems no ray on pride bestow,
"And latent metals innocently glow."

With weary steps, we rise up *Brandon*'s hill,
Where gazing wonder hath her utmost fill;
All *Bristol*'s city underneath it lies
Its reddening towers at once before your eyes.

From *Tindal*'s charming villa we descend,
To where resides the poet and the friend,
Where genius lives; where taste and wit combine;
Where fancy wantons with the tuneful Nine.
Oh, *More!* a muse to paint thy generous heart,
"Must catch a grace beyond the reach of art,"
Devoid of pedantry, thy numbers flow,
And sweet instruction with delight bestow:
The rough, unpolished manners you refine,
For sense and sensibility are thine;
All those sweet courtesies that friendship loves,
All that the heart susceptible approves,
Spontaneous flow with such peculiar grace
As time from memory can ne'er efface:
"O be thou blest with all that heaven can send,
"Long life, long health, long pleasure, and a friend!"

WILLIAM HEARD 1778

(From)

CLIFTON HILL

Ye silent, solemn, strong stupendous heights,
Whose terror-stalking frown the school-boy frights
From the young daw; whilst in your rugged breast
The chattering brood, secured by Horror, rest
Say, Muse, what arm the low'ring brothers cleft,
And the calm stream in this low cradle left?
Coeval with Creation they look down,
And, sunder'd, still retain their native frown.
Beneath those heights, lo! balmy springs arise,
To which pale Beauty's faded image flies;
Their kindly powers life's genial heat restore,
The tardy pulse, whose throbs were almost o'er,
Here beats a livelier tune. The breezy air,
To the wild hills invites the languid fair:
Fear not the western gale, thou tim'rous maid,
Nor dread its blast shall thy soft form invade;
Tho' cool and strong the quick'ning breezes blow,
And meet thy panting breath, 'twill quickly grow
More strong; then drink the odoriferous draught,
With unseen particles of health 'tis fraught.

ANN YEARSLEY 1786

TO MR. RUXTON

Prince's Buildings,
Clifton.
Dec. 29, 1791

MY DEAR UNCLE—If you are going to the canal put this letter in your pocket, and do not be troubled in your conscience about reading it, but keep it till you are perfectly at leisure: for I have nothing strange or new to tell you. We live just the same kind of life that we used to do at Edgeworthstown; and though we move amongst numbers, are not moved by them, but feel independent of them for our daily amusement. All the *phantasmas* I had conjured up to frighten myself, vanished after I had been here a week, for I found that they were but phantoms of my imagination, as you very truly told me. We live very near the Downs, where we have almost every day charming walks, and all the children go bounding about over hill and dale along with us. My aunt told me that once when you were at Clifton, when full dressed to go to a ball at Bath, you suddenly changed your mind, and undressed again, to go out a walking with her, and now that I see the walks, I am not surprised, even if you were not to have had the pleasure of my aunt's company. My father has got a *transfer* of a ticket for the Bristol library, which is an extremely fine one; and what makes it appear ten times finer is, that it is very difficult for strangers to get into. From thence he can get almost any book for us he pleases, except a few of the most scarce, which are by the laws of the library immovable. No ladies go to the library, but Mr. Johns, the librarian, is very civil, and my mother went to his rooms and saw the beautiful prints in Boydell's Shakespear.

MARIA EDGEWORTH 1791

(From)

KINGSWESTON HILL

Now, as I gradual climb the stately height,
The bursting prospect rushes on the sight:
Below, rich woods o'ershade the circled green,
Meads smile o'er meads, and gladden all the scene;
The streaky Severn changes on the sight,
Waving to beams of many-colour'd light;
O'er the clear main dispers'd, the less'ning sail,
(Thy wealth, proud Bristol!) dances in the gale:
Beyond, the Cambrian mountains dimly rise,
Point their blue tops, and vanish in the skies.
Approaching Autumn just begins to tinge
The leafy verdure with a golden fringe;
Thro' the fair scene unequal shades appear,
That speak the downfall of the waining year;
The fading foliage of the darksome pine,
The shrubby pool, where drooping osiers twine;
O'er the green bank the yellower flowrets shed,
And the late rose, that spots the copse with red;
The woodbine's feath'ry bloom, that, unconfin'd,
Mounts in the circles of the wafting wind;
While, 'midst his subject trees, the laden oak,
Tow'rs high, and casts beneath a kingly look.
Between his low-brow'd cliffs, and arching woods,
The gentle Avon rolls his fairy floods;
Pale ivy's wreaths embrace the moul'dring tow'r,
And swallows roost, where princes lodg'd before.

Thrice happy Bristol! whom such feats surround;
But happier still, for ev'ry muse renown'd!
Still shall thy vales with richest verdure shine,
Still the green laurel o'er thy forehead twine;
From age to age shall CHATTERTON survive,
While gen'rous sensibility shall live;
Command the breast to throb, the tear to flow,
In soft vicissitude of pleasing woe;
The echoing soul with rising fury move,
Sink to despair, or liquidate to love.

See where the silver adder welt'ring lies,
His speckled beauties trailing as he dies!
No more his eyes a fiery crimson boast,
Dim is their lustre, and their magic lost.
Thus is proud *Man* arrested in his way,
The gilded reptile of a longer day!
The great, the fair, resign their petty reign,
Vain their ambition, and their beauty vain.

THOMAS HOBHOUSE 1785

(From 'Aella')

MYNSTRELLES SONGE

O! synge untoe mie roundelaie,
O! droppe the brynie teare wythe mee,
Daunce ne moe atte hallie daie,
Lycke a reynynge ryver bee;
  Mie love ys dedde,
  Gon to hys death-bedde,
  Al under the wyllowe tree.

Blacke hys cryne as the wyntere nyghte,
Whyte hys rode as the sommer snowe,
Rodde hys face as the mornynge lyghte,
Cale he lyes ynne the grave belowe;
  Mie love ys dedde,
  Gon to hys deathe-bedde,
  Al under the wyllowe tree.

Swote hys tyngue as the throstles note,
Quycke ynn daunce as thoughte canne bee,
Defte hys taboure, codgelle stote,
O! hee lyes bie the wyllowe tree:
  Mie love ys dedde,
  Gonne to hys deathe-bedde,
  Alle underre the wyllowe tree.

Harke! the ravenne flappes hys wynge,
In the briered delle belowe;
Harke! the dethe-owle loude dothe synge,
To the nyghte-mares as heie goe;
  Mie love ys dedde,
  Gonne to hys deathe-bedde,
  Al under the wyllowe tree.

See! the whyte moone sheenes onne hie;
Whyterre ys mie true loves shroude;
Whyterre yanne the mornynge skie,
Whyterre yanne the evenynge cloude;
  Mie love ys dedde,
  Gon to hys deathe-bedde,
  Al under the wyllowe tree.

Heere, uponne mie true loves grave,
Schalle the baren fleurs be layde,
Nee one hallie Seyncte to save
Al the celness of a mayde.
  Mie love ys dedde,
  Gonne to hys death-bedde,
  Alle under the wyllowe tree.

Wythe mie hondes I'lle dente the brieres
Rounde his hallie corse to gre,
Ouphante fairie, lyghte youre fyres,
Heere mie boddie stylle schalle bee.
  Mie love ys dedde,
  Gon to hys death-bedde,
  Al under the wyllowe tree.

Comme, wythe acorne-coppe and thorne,
Drayne mie hartys blodde awaie;
Lyfe and all yttes goode I scorne,
Daunce bie nete, or feaste by daie.
  Mie love ys dedde,
  Gon to hys death-bedde,
  Al under the wyllowe tree.

T. CHATTERTON 1769

[*'Stay curyous Traveller and pass not bye'*]

Stay curyous Traveller and pass not bye
Until this fetive Pile astounde thine Eye
Whole Rocks on Rocks with Yron joynd surveie
And Okes with Okes entremed disponed lie
This mightie Pile that keeps the Wyndes at Baie
Fyre Levin and the mokie Storme defie
That shootes aloofe into the Reaulmes of daie
Shall be the Record of the Buylders Fame for aie

Thou seest this Maystrie of a human hand
The Pride of Brystowe and the Westerne Lande
Yet is the Buylders Vertues much moe greete
Greeter than can bie Rowlie's Pen be scande—
Thou seest the Saynctes and Kynges in Stonen State
That seemd with Breath and human Soule dispande
As payrde to us enseem these Men of State
Such is greete Canynge's mynde when payrd to God elate

Well maiest thou be astound but view it well
Go not from hence before thou see thy fill
And learn the Builder's Vertues and his name
Of this tall Spyre in every Countye telle
And with thy Tale the lazing Rychmen shame
Showe howe the Glorious Canynge did excelle
How hee good Man a Friend for Kynges became
And gloryous paved at once the Waie to Heavn and Fame

T. CHATTERTON 1768

ELEGY [I]

Haste, haste, ye solemn messengers of night,
Spread the black mantle on the shrinking plain;
But, ah! my torments still survive the light,
The changing seasons alter not my pain.

Ye variegated children of the spring;
Ye blossoms blushing with the pearly dew;
Ye birds that sweetly in the hawthorn sing;
Ye flow'ry meadows; lawns of verdant hue,

Faint are your colours; harsh your love-notes thrill;
To me no pleasure nature now can yield:
Alike the barren rock and woody hill,
The dark-brown blasted heath, and fruitful field.

Ye spouting cataracts, ye silver streams;
Ye spacious rivers, whom the willow shrouds,
Ascend the bright-crown'd sun's far-shining beams,
To aid the mournful tear-distilling clouds,

Ye circling seasons, intercept the year;
Forbid the beauties of the spring to rise,
Let not the life-preserving grain appear;
Let howling tempests harrow up the skies.

Ye cloud-girt, moss-grown turrets, look no more
Into the palace of the God of day:
Ye loud tempestuous billows, cease to roar,
In plaintive numbers, thro' the valleys stray.

Ye verdant-vested trees, forget to grow,
Cast off the yellow foliage of your pride:
Ye softly-tinkling riv'lets, cease to flow,
Or swell'd with certain death and poison, glide.

Ye solemn warblers of the gloomy night,
That rest in lightning-blasted oaks the day,
Thro' the black mantles take your slow-pac'd flight,
Rending the silent wood with shrieking lay.

Ye snow-crown'd mountains lost to mortal eyes,
Down to the valleys bend your hoary head.
Ye livid comets, fire the peopled skies,
For lady Betty's tabby cat is dead.

T. CHATTERTON, BRISTOL — 4th April, 1769

(From)

CLIFTON

Clifton, sweet village! now demands the lay,
The lov'd retreat of all the rich and gay;
The darling spot which pining maidens seek,
To give Health's roses to the pallid cheek.
Warm from its font the holy water pours,
And lures the sick to Clifton's neighbouring bowers.
Let bright Hygeia her glad reign resume,
And o'er each sickly form renew her bloom.
Me, whom no fell disease this hour compels
To visit Bristol's celebrated Wells,
Far other motives prompt my eager view,
My Heart can here its fav'rite bent pursue;
Here can I gaze, and pause, and muse between,
And draw some moral truth from ev'ry scene.

Yon dusky rocks, that from the stream arise
In rude rough grandeur, threat the distant skies,
Seem as if Nature in a painful throe,
With dire convulsions lab'ring to and fro,
(To give the boiling waves a ready vent)
At one dread stroke the solid mountain rent,
The huge cleft rocks transmit to distant fame,
The sacred gilding of a good Saint's name.

Now Brandon's cliffs my wand'ring gazes meet,
Whose craggy surface mocks the ling'ring feet;
Queen Bess's gift (so antient legends say)
To Bristol's fair; where to the sun's warm ray
On the rough bush the linen white they spread,
Or deck with russet leaves the mossy bed.

Eager at length I strain each aching limb,
And breathless now the mountain's summit climb.
Here does Attention her fixt gaze renew,
And of the city takes a nearer view.
The yellow Avon, creeping at my side,
In sullen billows rolls a muddy tide;
No sportive Naiads on her streams are seen,
No chearful pastimes deck the gloomy scene;
Fixt in a stupor by the chearless plain,
Her fairy flights the fancy toils in vain:
For tho' her waves, by commerce richly blest,
Roll to her shores the treasures of the West,
Tho' her broad banks Trade's busy aspect wears,
She seems unconscious of the wealth she bears.

T. CHATTERTON — July 1769

BETSY OF THE HILL

If gentle Love's immortal fire
  Could animate the quill,
Soon should the rapture-speaking lyre
  Sing Betsy of the Hill.

My beating heart incessant moves,
  No interval 'tis still,
And all my ravish'd Nature loves
  Sweet Betsy of the Hill.

Her dying, soft, expressive eye,
  Her elegance, must kill;
Ye Gods! how many thousands die
  For Betsy of the Hill.

A graceful look, majestic air,
  A sentiment, a skill,
In all the graces of the fair,
  Mark Betsy of the Hill.

Thou mighty power, eternal Fate,
  My happiness to fill,
O bless a wretched lover's state
  With Betsy of the Hill.

T. CHATTERTON — June 1770

EPITAPH

FOR A PROPOSED MONUMENT TO CHATTERTON,* AT BRISTOL

Pause, Stranger! this recording marble bears
  The name of Chatterton! Few sons of woe
E'er past Life's sojourn, press'd with heavier cares,
  Or felt, more oft, the tear, in darkness, flow.

Though *Genius* nursed him as her darling child,
  And, round his brow, her choicest wreaths entwined,
Neglect turn'd, heedless, from his warblings wild,
  And, far from friend and home, with *want* he pined!

Sighs now avail not! yet, a grateful age
  Bestows the last poor *meed* that still remains,
This Tablet, less enduring than his page,
  And gives him *back* his own transcendent strains.

*A year or two ago, it was the writer's wish, by means of a Public Subscription, to raise a monument to Chatterton. Upon applying, however, to the Dean of Bristol for his sanction, he informed him (through a friend) that the circumstances of Chatterton's *death* would operate as an effectual bar to any such monument being placed in the *Cathedral*.

J. COTTLE — 1800

(From)

BRISTOLIA: A POEM

Majestic Bristol! to thy happy port
Prolific COMMERCE makes its lov'd resort;
Thy gallant ships, with spacious sails, unfurl'd,
Waft, to thy shore, the treasures of the world!
With each production of the East, and West,
Thy favor'd citizens are amply blest;
Thy active sons, unceasingly, are sway'd
By HONOR, JUSTICE, and a thirst for TRADE;

Lo! mid the spacious walks of COLLEGE-GREEN,
What num'rous crowds of blooming nymphs are seen!
Beneath the branches of th' extended trees,
They take their circuit, and imbibe the breeze.
Not HELEN's face, which prov'd the fall of TROY,
Outshone the charms BRISTOLIA's FAIR enjoy;
With these, DIANA, and her virgin train,
May vie for beauty, but, may vie in vain;
Nor VENUS' self, were VENUS to appear,
Could look, in figure, or in face, more fair:
The graceful form, with rapture, I survey;
And piercing eyes, where sportive Cupids play:
The swelling breast, more white than Alpine snow,
Where HONOR triumphs, and the VIRTUES grow;
In charms, like these, *Bristolia's daughters* shine,
And boast a semblance equal to divine.

To BRANDON HILL my journey I pursue,
From whence BRISTOLIA forms a pleasing view.
Now, on its summit, as I, musing, stray,
I trace the spot where hostile Britons lay;
But *discord*, now, and *civil wars*, are o'er,
And joy, and *commerce*, bless BRISTOLIA's shore:
Now, from each quarter, clouds of smoke appear,
Mount their black columns, and dissolve in air;
Buildings superb, and lofty spires, surprise
The gazer's senses, and enchant his eyes;
Whilst, to his ears, in quick vibration, come
The noise of trucks, and city's ceaseless hum:
The shouts of sailors, as their castles ride,
With waving streamers, on the chrystal tide;
All which declare, to Bristol's busy throng
That *commerce*, *wealth*, and *industry* belong.

ROMAINE JOSEPH THORN 1794

(From)

BRISTOL: A SATIRE

Low in a drear and gloomy Vale immur'd,
By mud cemented, and by smoke obscur'd,
A City stands, and BRISTOL is its name,
By trade and dullness consecrate to fame,
That o'er her Sons in form of Plutus reigns,
And binds their groveling hearts in golden chains;
This to their brain a leaden mask imparts,
And makes their heads as callous as their hearts.

In mingled heaps here mud and misery lie,
Here vice and folly rear their standard high;
Here sweating dustman, sweating dustman meets,
But all their efforts ne'er can cleanse their streets,
While heedless Magistrates recline in peace,
Content to mumble o'er the good Police
But ne'er essay its blessings to secure,
Nor stretch the hand to help the suppliant poor;
Suffice to them the *name*, the important air,
The *Fur-Clad Gown* and *Magisterial Chair*.
Hail! BRISTOL hail! and hail thy "busy throng"
Whom thine own bard has famed in matchless song,
Thy Thorn for thee has tun'd the trembling string,
And bade his Muse in lofty notes to sing.
How sweet the lay which gives thy charms to fame,
How sweetly classic thy poetic name:
BRISTOL no more a vulgar sound we hear,
But soft BRISTOLIA soothes the list'ning ear;
Or if per chance, the gothic word we trace,
'Tis dubb'd "Majestic" and assumes a grace,

Ev'n on this theme, 'twere easier far to dwell
Than praise the City which thou lov'st so well;
Easier than proving (which thy strains presume)
That BRISTOL wears the form of ancient Rome.
That all her streets are *grand* beyond compare,
Her Sons all *gen'rous* and her Daughters *fair*.
BRISTOL in thee has dullness fixed her throne,
(Congenial seat) and marks thy Sons her own;
On thee the Goddess cast her cloudy eyes,
And saw sublime thy welcome fogs arise;

From Owl-like sleep, with secret joy awoke,
Pleased with the incense of thy curling smoke.
To guard her laws, and aid her mighty reign
All-powerful Plutus fills the busy brain;
Full oft the God inspires the golden dream
Of cent per cent, and many a goodly scheme:
In all his Sons the mystic signs we trace,
Pounds, Shillings, Pence appear in every face.
Here worth is prized, if worth will *aught* obtain,
And truth is judg'd by rules of *loss* and *gain*.
The love of virtue's lost in love of pence
And mean, low cunning holds the place of sense.

Majestic Goddess who dost rule supreme
Thy favorite City and its *muddy* stream;
A ditch, a stagnant pool, a lazy flood,
A rill slow creeping through a world of mud.
Thou who did'st bid thy *Thorn* his verse produce,
And spoil the paper meant for better use.
Long hast thou held illimitable power,
And crush'd young merit in its rising hour.

Here let me pause o'er genius' hapless Son,
Here drop the pensive tear for CHATTERTON.
Ill-fated youth whose proud yet gen'rous Soul,
Glowing with ardor spurn'd the base controul;
He saw the Sons of wealth in pamper'd pride,
He saw the poor the scanty boon denied;
Saw vice ennobled on its titled seat,
While worth unfriended sought a lone retreat;
He saw proud folly catch the admiring eye,
And modest genius unreguarded die:
He felt that justice from the world was driv'n
And rush'd to meet her in her native heav'n.

Return oh! Muse to BRISTOL's matchless Sons,
In avarice *Dutchmen*, and in science *Huns*.
Trade, mighty trade, here holds resistless sway,
And drives the nobler cares of *mind* away.
To this sole object every effort tends,
And virtue dies and *pliant* honor bends;
No soft humanities are cherish'd here,
No sympathetic feeling prompts the tear;
No mild urbanity attracts the fight,

No arts of skill or elegant delight;
But sordid wealth inspires the general cry,
And speeds the step and sharps the eager eye;
Foul as their streets, triumphant meanness sways,
And grov'ling as their mud-compelling drays;
Discordant sounds compose the babel hum,
'Tis "how goes sugar? what's the price of rum?"
"What ships arrived? and how are stocks to-day?"
"Who's dead? who's broken? and who's run away?"

These constant cares with constant gain requite;
Hence BRISTOL boasts full many a wealthy wight;
Yet not benevolence is here display'd,
No generous impulse warms the sons of trade:
Avarice *first* taught the golden store to *heap*,
Her *next* great lesson is that store to *keep*.

Thus through the series of full many an age,
(Annals of infamy) her blushing page
Records alone *one* solitary name,
To generous virtue dear, and dear to fame;
Benevolence gladden'd at her COLSTON's fight,
And sickening avarice sought the realms of night;
He fear'd the bright example might inspire,
His chosen children with the gen'rous fire;
But fear not, BRISTOL shall uphold thy state,
Tho' all shall *praise* him, none shall *imitate!*

From distant realms, the mighty vessels fraught,
From either zone the native product's brought;
But chief the western isles attention gain,
Where grows the saccharine and juicy cane:
Wide spreads the sail from BRISTOL's busy quay,
To Afric's coast directs the eager way,
Their motive avarice, and trade their plan,
Their means oppression, and their commerce man.
The hapless victim sold to till the soil,
Reaps only misery for his lengthened toil;
To us the grateful plant is freely given,
A feast unguilty by the hand of heav'n;
But the sad slave the unblest produce rears,
"Fans with his sighs, and waters with his tears"
Thus man perverts what heav'n intended good,
And dies the growing plant with human blood;
Slaves torn and mangled, cultivate the sweet,
That trade may thrive, and luxury may eat.

ROBERT LOVELL 1794

THE EBB TIDE

Slowly thy flowing tide
Came in, old Avon! scarcely did mine eyes,
As watchfully I roam'd thy green-wood side,
Perceive its gentle rise.

With many a stroke and strong
The labouring boatmen upward plied their oars,
Yet little way they made, though labouring long
Between they winding shores.

Now down thine ebbing tide
The unlabour'd boat falls rapidly along;
The solitary helm's-man sits to guide,
And sings an idle song.

Now o'er the rocks that lay
So silent late, the shallow current roars;
Fast flow thy waters on their seaward way
Through wider-spreading shores.

Avon! I gaze and know
The lesson emblem'd in thy varying way;
It speaks of human joys that rise so slow,
So rapidly decay.

Kingdoms which long have stood,
And slow to strength and power attain'd at last,
Thus from the summit of high fortune's flood
They ebb to ruin fast.

Thus like thy flow appears
Time's tardy course to manhood's envied stage;
Alas! how hurryingly the ebbing years
Then hasten to old age!

R. SOUTHEY — Westbury, 1799

TO A GOOSE

If thou didst feed on western plains of yore;
Or waddle wide with flat and flabby feet
Over some Cambrian mountain's plashy moor;
Or find in farmer's yard a safe retreat
From gipsy thieves, and foxes sly and fleet;
If thy grey quills, by lawyer guided, trace
Deeds big with ruin to some wretched race,
Or love-sick poet's sonnet, sad and sweet,
Wailing the rigour of his lady fair;
Or if, the drudge of housemaid's daily toil,
Cobwebs and dust thy pinions white besoil,
Departed Goose! I neither know nor care.
But this I know, that we pronounced thee fine,
Season'd with sage and onions, and port wine.

R. SOUTHEY — 1795

SONNET VI

As slow and solemn yonder deepening knell
Tolls through the sullen evening's shadowy gloom,
Alone and pensive, in my silent room,
On man and on mortality I dwell.
And as the harbinger of death I hear
Frequent and full, much do I love to muse
On life's distemper'd scenes of hope and fear;
And passion varying her camelion hues,
And man pursuing pleasure's empty shade,
'Till death dissolves the vision. So the child
In youth's gay morn with wondering pleasure smil'd,
As with the shining ice well-pleas'd he play'd;
Nor, as he grasps the crystal in his play,
Heeds how the faithless bauble melts away.

R. SOUTHEY 1794

COMPOSED WHILE CLIMBING THE LEFT ASCENT OF BROCKLEY COOMB, SOMERSETSHIRE, MAY 1795

With many a pause and oft reverted eye
I climb the Coomb's ascent: sweet songsters near
Warble in shade their wild-wood melody:
Far off the unvarying Cuckoo soothes my ear.
Up scour the startling stragglers of the flock
That on green plots o'er precipices browze:
From the deep fissures of the naked rock
The Yew-tree bursts! Beneath its dark green boughs
(Mid which the May-thorn blends its blossoms white)
Where broad smooth stones jut out in mossy seats,
I rest:—and now have gain'd the topmost site.
Ah! what a luxury of landscape meets
My gaze! Proud towers , and Cots more dear to me,
Elm-shadow'd Fields, and prospect-bounding Sea!
Deep sighs my lonely heart: I drop the tear:
Enchanting spot! O were my Sara here!

S. T. COLERIDGE 1795

TINTERN ABBEY

"No poem of mine was composed under circumstances more pleasant for me to remember than this. I began it upon leaving Tintern, after crossing the Wye, and concluded it just as I was entering Bristol in the evening, after a ramble of four or five days with my sister. Not a word of it was altered and not any part of it written down till I reached Bristol." [The poem was included in 'The Lyrical Ballads' which Joseph Cottle was to print.]—WILLIAM WORDSWORTH.

COMPOSED A FEW MILES ABOVE TINTERN ABBEY, ON REVISITING THE BANKS OF THE WYE DURING A TOUR. JULY 13, 1798

Five years have past; five summers, with the length
Of five long winters! and again I hear
These waters, rolling from their mountain-springs
With a soft inland murmur.—Once again
Do I behold these steep and lofty cliffs,
That on a wild secluded scene impress
Thoughts of more deep seclusion; and connect
The landscape with the quiet of the sky.
The day is come when I again repose
Here, under this dark sycamore, and view
These plots of cottage-ground, these orchard-tufts,
Which at this season, with their unripe fruits,
Are clad in one green hue, and lose themselves
'Mid groves and copses. Once again I see
These hedge-rows, hardly hedge-rows, little lines
Of sportive wood run wild: these pastoral farms,
Green to the very door; and wreaths of smoke
Sent up, in silence, from among the trees,
With some uncertain notice, as might seem,
Of vagrant dwellers in the houseless woods,
Or of some hermit's cave, where by his fire
The hermit sits alone.
Though absent long,
These forms of beauty have not been to me,
As is a landscape to a blind man's eye:
But oft, in lonely rooms, and mid the din
Of towns and cities, I have owed to them,
In hours of weariness, sensations sweet,
Felt in the blood, and felt along the heart,
And passing even into my purer mind
With tranquil restoration—feelings too
Of unremembered pleasure; such, perhaps,
As may have had no trivial influence
On that best portion of a good man's life;

His little, nameless, unremembered acts
Of kindness and of love. Nor less, I trust,
To them I may have owed another gift,
Of aspect more sublime; that blessed mood,
In which the burthen of the mystery,
In which the heavy and the weary weight
Of all this unintelligible world
Is lighten'd:—that serene and blessed mood,
In which the affections gently lead us on,
Until, the breath of this corporeal frame,
And even the motion of our human blood
Almost suspended, we are laid asleep
In body, and become a living soul:
While with an eye made quiet by the power
Of harmony, and the deep power of joy,
We see into the life of things.

If this
Be but a vain belief, yet, oh! how oft,
In darkness, and amid the many shapes
Of joyless day-light; when the fretful stir
Unprofitable, and the fever of the world,
Have hung upon the beatings of my heart,
How oft, in spirit, have I turned to thee
O sylvan Wye! Thou wanderer through the woods,
How often has my spirit turned to thee!
And now, with gleams of half-extinguish'd thought,
With many recognitions dim and faint,
And somewhat of a sad perplexity,
The picture of the mind revives again:
While here I stand, not only with the sense
Of present pleasure, but with pleasing thoughts
That in this moment there is life and food
For future years. And so I dare to hope
Though changed, no doubt, from what I was, when first
I came among these hills; when like a roe
I bounded o'er the mountains, by the sides
Of the deep rivers, and the lonely streams,
Wherever nature led; more like a man
Flying from something that he dreads, than one
Who sought the thing he loved. For nature then
(The coarser pleasures of my boyish days,
And their glad animal movements all gone by,)
To me was all in all.—I cannot paint
What then I was, The sounding cataract
Haunted me like a passion: the tall rock,

The mountain, and the deep and gloomy wood,
Their colours and their forms, were then to me
An appetite: a feeling and a love,
That had no need of a remoter charm,
By thought supplied, or any interest
Unborrowed from the eye.—That time is past,
And all its aching joys are now no more,
And all its dizzy raptures. Not for this
Faint I, nor mourn nor murmur: other gifts
Have followed, for such loss, I would believe,
Abundant recompence. For I have learned
To look on nature, not as in the hour
Of thoughtless youth, but hearing oftentimes
The still, sad music of humanity,
Not harsh nor grating, though of ample power
To chasten and subdue. And I have felt
A presence that disturbs me with the joy
Of elevated thoughts; a sense sublime
Of something far more deeply interfused,
Whose dwelling is the light of setting suns,
And the round ocean, and the living air,
And the blue sky, and in the mind of man,
A motion and a spirit, that impels
All thinking things, all objects of all thought,
And rolls through all things. Therefore am I still
A lover of the meadows and the woods,
And mountains; and of all that we behold
From this green earth; of all the mighty world
Of eye and ear, both what they half-create,
And what perceive; well pleased to recognize
In nature and the language of the sense,
The anchor of my purest thoughts, the nurse,
The guide, the guardian of my heart, and soul
Of all my moral being.

Nor, perchance,
If I were not thus taught, should I the more
Suffer my genial spirits to decay:
For thou art with me, here, upon the banks
Of this fair river; thou, my dearest Friend,

My dear, dear Friend, and in thy voice I catch
The language of my former heart, and read
My former pleasures in the shooting lights
Of thy wild eyes. Oh! yet a little while
May I behold in thee what I was once,
My dear, dear Sister! And this prayer I make,
Knowing that Nature never did betray
The heart that loved her; 'tis her privilege,
Through all the years of this our life, to lead
From joy to joy: for she can so inform
The mind that is within us, so impress
With quietness and beauty, and so feed
With lofty thoughts, that neither evil tongues,
Rash judgments, nor the sneers of selfish men,
Nor greetings where no kindness is, nor all
The dreary intercourse of daily life,
Shall e'er prevail against us, or disturb
Our chearful faith that all which we behold
Is full of blessings. Therefore let the moon
Shine on thee in thy solitary walk;
And let the misty mountain winds be free
To blow against thee: and in after years,
When these wild ecstasies shall be matured
Into a sober pleasure, when thy mind
Shall be a mansion for all lovely forms,

Thy memory be as a dwelling-place
For all sweet sounds and harmonies; Oh! then,
If solitude, or fear, or pain, or grief,
Should be thy portion, with what healing thoughts
Of tender joy wilt thou remember me,
And these my exhortations! Nor, perchance,
If I should be, where I no more can hear
Thy voice, nor catch from thy wild eyes these gleams
Of past existence, wilt thou then forget
That on the banks of this delightful stream
We stood together; and that I so long
A worshipper of Nature, hither came,
Unwearied in that service: rather say
With warmer love, oh! with far deeper zeal
Of holier love. Nor wilt thou then forget,
That after many wanderings, many years
Of absence, these steep woods and lofty cliffs,
And this green pastoral landscape, were to me
More dear, both for themselves, and for thy sake.

W. WORDSWORTH 1798

(From)

LONG ASHTON

Now lab'ring up the steep I climb
Till from the fir-crown'd height sublime,
Earth's beauteous scene, opes to the eye,
With all the vast expanded sky.—
The circling hills with sweeping swell,
Slope to many a lonely dell,
The Park, with all the Woodland green,
The Mansion through the foliage seen,
And dwellings group'd, and scatter'd cot,
Afar, the boundless Landscape dot!

O come, whom Nature's scenes invite,
Rove this green hill, with footsteps light,
And rural vales thine eye shall charm,
And Views sublime thy feelings warm!
Or should the sun with ardour glow,
Haste to the shelter'd Lane below,
Where verdant hedges screen from heat,
And stroll mid banks of vi'lets sweet;
Until thy wand'ring step invades
Green Yanley's calm sequester'd glades,
With cot, and vale, and wood, and hill,
And song of Birds, and babbling rill:
Or where swift Ashton-water clear
Sweet sounding to the list'ning ear,
Retir'd afar from busy crowds,
In shaded Dells, its streamlet shrouds:
Where Gatcomb spreads its hamlet green
With all its rustick Charms unseen—
Or o'er Bower Ashton's meadows stray
And Nature's Landscape rich survey;
Where green with Shrubs yon Mansion stands
That all the wat'ry Scene commands;
Or view the Cliff's majestick break,—
When spreads the tide, like tranquil Lake,—
With some light Sloop's expanded Sail,—
Borne o'er its bosom by the gale.—

From Cot retir'd, and peaceful glen,
The Muse turns to the haunts of Men,
Where Bristol, gay with masts and spires,
Glows with the golden solar Fires—

Spread o'er the Down, the mingled Throng
In gayest colours move along—
Some rambling o'er the lofty hill,
Crown'd by ruins of the Mill.
And some, to join the crowded scene,
Winding the path, the Cliffs between;
While Music, soul inspiring sound,
Breathes sweet enchantment all around,
Steals through the windings of the Dell,
Mounts the tall Cliff with sounding swell;
Till Leigh's green wood returns the strain,
In Echoes soften'd, back again.—

Now roves the eye across the flood,
To yon bold Mansion, bower'd in wood,
The Cottage peeping from the glade,
The cluster'd Fir-trees, dark in shade,
And all the verdant slope below
Touch'd by the Sun with golden glow;
Where thick the Flock collected rest
Beneath the shading Elms' green Crest;
And seem a tranquil bliss to share
Devoid of every future care—
So Childhood tastes the present joy,
Nor thought of ills unfelt annoy;
For grief that moistens youthful eyes
Is like the shower from April skies,
When clouds pass dark'ning on their way
Succeeded by the sunny ray;
And Nature's lovely face appears
As if a Smile illum'd her Tears.—

O! who amid these Scenes can rove,
Nor mingled awe and wonder prove!
Stupendous slopes, with woodland pride,
Green to the margin of the Tide!
Now rugged rocks that high in air,
Lift their dark Forms of verdure bare!
How bold yon cliff uprears his head,
The fabled Giant's cavern'd Bed!
And that which rises by the side,
Grac'd by the Ivy's verdant pride,
In all his rude primeval charm,
Untouch'd by Man's destructive Arm!

Oft Fashion's polish'd Votaries stray,
Beneath these rocks in colours gay;
Retiring from the splendid scene,
To simple Nature's charms serene.
For many a joyless heart is found,
Revolving in gay Pleasure's round—
The crowded Rout, the Play, the Ball,
Will on the listless Gazer pall,
And midst profusion's glare, the breast
Still sighs for something unpossess'd.

How silent all the scene around!
E'en yon huge City's mingled sound,
With all her varied cares opprest
Appears as hush'd in tranquil rest.—
The Soldiers' march extended far,
With glitt'ring arms, and pomp of war,
In measur'd steps, that sounding fall—
To the loud Drum and Fife's shrill Call,—
And gather'd Crowd, that press to view,—
Or wide with hurried steps pursue.—
Her bustling Port, where commerce reigns
That wafts from ev'ry Clime her gains,
With freighted Ships, their close bent sails,
In rest from Ocean's sweeping gales—
Rich Merchandise from distant Isles,
Outspread afar in ample Piles,
And ratling Cart, and silent Dray,
Thick moving on their busy way.—
The passing Crowd, that ceaseless glide,
Swift down the Street, a living tide—
Where life displays each changeful stage,
From blooming youth, to wither'd age—
The grave, the gay, the haughty air,
That Brow opprest with wrinkled Care;
The hurrying Tradesman's busy face,
The Idler, strolling with slow pace,
The tatter'd garb, that Want betrays,
Proud wealth, that splendid state displays;
And Beauty, glancing on the eye,
And with the crowd swift passing by:
Whose countless numbers onward move,
Like billows o'er the Ocean rove.

W. MORGAN 1814

DREAM-PEDLARY

If there were dreams to sell,
  What would you buy?
Some cost a passing bell;
  Some a light sigh,
That shakes from Life's fresh crown
Only a roseleaf down.
If there were dreams to sell,
Merry and sad to tell,
And the crier rung the bell,
  What would you buy?

A cottage lone and still,
  With bowers nigh,
Shadowy, my woes to still,
  Until I die.
Such pearl from Life's fresh crown
Fain would I shake me down.
Were dreams to have at will,
This would best heal my ill,
  This would I buy.

But there were dreams to sell,
  Ill didst thou buy;
Life is a dream, they tell,
  Waking, to die.
Dreaming a dream to prize,
Is wishing ghosts to rise;
  And, if I had the spell
  To call the buried, well,
  Which one would I?

If there are ghosts to raise,
  What shall I call,
Out of hell's murky haze,
  Heaven's blue hall?
Raise my loved longlost boy
To lead me to his joy.
  There are no ghosts to raise;
  Out of death lead no ways;
  Vain is the call.

Know'st thou not ghosts to sue?
  No love thou hast.
Else lie, as I will do,
  And breathe thy last.
So out of Life's fresh crown
Fall like a rose-leaf down.
  Thus are the ghosts to woo;
  Thus are all dreams made true,
  Ever to last!

T. L. BEDDOES 1826–29

THE GHOSTS' MOONSHINE

It is midnight, my wedded;
  Let us lie under
The tempest bright, my dreaded,
  In the warm thunder:
Tremble and weep not! What can you fear?
  My heart's best wish is thine,—
That thou wert white, and bedded
  On the softest bier,
  In the ghosts' moonshine.
  Is that the wind? No, no;
  Only two devils, that blow
  Through the murderer's ribs to and fro,
    In the ghosts' moonshine.

Who is there, she said afraid, yet
  Stirring and awaking
The poor old dead? His spade, it
  Is only making—
(Tremble and weep not! What do you crave?)
  Where yonder grasses twine,
A pleasant bed, my maid, that
  Children call a grave,
    In the cold moonshine.
  Is that the wind? No, no;
  Only two devils, that blow
  Through the murderer's ribs to and fro,
    In the ghosts' moonshine.

What dost thou strain above her
  Lovely throat's whitness?
A silken chain, to cover
  Her bosom's brightness?
Tremble and weep not: what dost thou fear?
  —My blood is spilt like wine,
Thou hast strangled and slain me, lover,
  Thou hast stabbed me, dear,
    In the ghosts' moonshine.
  Is that the wind? No, no;
  Only her goblin doth blow
  Through the murderer's ribs to and fro,
    In its own moonshine.

T. L. BEDDOES 1824–25

DIRGE

If thou wilt ease thine heart
Of love and all its smart,
    Then sleep, dear, sleep;
And not a sorrow
  Hang any tear on your eyelashes;
    Lie still and deep,
  Sad soul, until the sea-wave washes
The rim o' th' sun to-morrow,
    In eastern sky.

But wilt thou cure thy heart
Of love and all its smart,
    Then die, dear, die;
'Tis deeper, sweeter,
  Than on a rose bank to lie dreaming
    With folded eye;
  And then alone, amid the beaming
Of love's stars, thou'lt meet her
    In eastern sky.

SONG

How many times do I love thee, dear?
  Tell me how many thoughts there be
    In the atmosphere
    Of a new-fall'n year,
Whose white and sable hours appear
  The latest flake of Eternity:
So many times do I love thee, dear.

How many times do I love again?
  Tell me how many beads there are
    In a silver chain
    Of evening rain,
Unravelled from the tumbling main,
  And threading the eye of a yellow star:
So many times do I love again.

T. L. BEDDOES 1826–29

SONNET

ON THE CHURCH OF ST. MARY REDCLIFF, BRISTOL.

Tower! that like some old pyramid dost rear
  August thy massive pile, which lightning strook
In days of yore, while rolls this earthy sphere
  The ages of mankind shall on thee look.
For he, who, pacing lone the river-mead,
  Watch'd the sun's glory, that around thee shone,
With wild, enthusiast gaze, though dark his deed,
  Hath found in thee a monumental stone.
O marvellous boy! that pride was not of earth
  Which made thee bear all misery but scorn;
Thy inspirations were of heavenly birth,
  And fancy-tinted with the hues of morn;
Ev'n the writhen brow, that spoke thy fierce despair,
Told of th' immortal spirit prison'd there.

CHARLES ELTON 1835

TO THE RIVER AVON

Avon! why runnest thou away so fast?
Rest thee before that Chancel where repose
The bones of him whose spirit moves the world.
I have beheld thy birthplace, I have seen
Thy tiny ripples where they played amid
The golden cups and ever-waving blades.
I have seen mighty rivers, I have seen
Padus, recovered from his firy wound,
And Tiber, prouder than them all to bear
Upon his tawny bosom men who crusht
The world they trod on, heeding not the cries
Of culprit kings and nations many tongued.
What are to me these rivers, once adorn'd
With crowns they would not wear but swept away?
Worthier art thou of worship, and I bend
My knees upon thy bank, and call thy name,
And hear, or think I hear, thy voice reply.

W. S. LANDOR 1853

AVON RIVER

Ye rocks, and woods, and verdant scenes,
  That grace the banks of Avon river:
Great Nature's blessings on you rest,
  And your sweet beauty bloom for ever;
For there the Muse delighted roves,
  Now summer flowers are freely springing,
Enraptured with the tender songs
  The wild birds to their loves are singing.

The garden gay hath many charms,
  When bud and flower, care-cultur'd blossom:
The blushing rose, and lily pale,
  All fair and sweet as Venus' bosom;
But give me your sequester'd scenes,
  Your fields with richest verdure swelling,
Your groves, beneath whose friendly shade,
  The primrose makes her lowly dwelling.

For dearer is your simplest charm,
  Than aught vain labouring Art discloses;
And sweeter your green mossy banks,
  Than Luxury's rich bed of roses:
For here the soul, secure from strife,
  Can smile on Folly's vain ambition;
And scorn base Mammon's golden lure—
  Betraying thousands to perdition.

Some love the court, some love the field,
  Some love the trumpet's thund'ring rattle,
When chiefs contend for sov'reign power,
  And rival nations meet in battle;
But I, the Muse's humblest son—
  Blest be the great and good All-giver!—
Know not a wish beyond the scenes
  That grace the banks of Avon River.

JOHN JAMES 1841

A page from

'BRISTOL AND ITS FAMOUS ASSOCIATIONS'

In the month of May, 1845, the author of the *Ingoldsby Legends*, Rev. R. H. Barham, was living at 9 Dowry Square, in a vain effort to regain his shattered health. He gives a humorous sketch of his medical attendants during his stay. "If," says he, "In the multitude of counsellors there be wisdom, in that of apothecaries there is jaw, and with such a one as my adviser possesses, Samson might have laid waste all Mesopotamia, let alone Philistia. He has the art of saying nothing in a cascade of language comparable only to that 'almighty water privilege' —Niagara. In the bulletin written whilst here Barham cleverly hits off his medical attendants—

"Hark! the doctors come again,
Knock—and enter doctors twain—
Dr. Keeler, Dr. Blane:—
'Well, sir, how
Go matters now?
Please put out your tongue again!'
Meanwhile t'other side the bed,
Dr. Keeler
Is a feeler
Of my wrist, and shakes his head:—
'Rather low, we are rather low!'

" 'Now, what sort of night, sir, eh?
Did you take the mixture, pray?
Iodine and anodyne,
Ipecacuanha wine,
And the draught and pills at nine?'

Patient (*loquitur*).

" 'Coughing, doctor, coughing, sneezing,
Wheezing, teasing, most unpleasing,
Till at length I, by degrees, in-
Duced "Tired nature's sweet restorer,"
Sleep, to cast her mantle o'er her
Poor unfortunate adorer,
And became at last a snorer.' "

The last piece this genial humorist ever wrote—*As I Lay a Thynkynge* —was written at the Hotwells. Finding himself no better for his stay, he returned home, and on the 17th of June, 1845, he passed away.

STANLEY HUTTON 1907

(From)

BRISTOWA'S PROPHECY

"Oh, Bristol! my darling! the pride of your youth,
  Is fled like the dream of a maiden's first love,
When your heart was all burning for glory and truth,
  And your fancy was bright as the star-beams above.

It is gone, and for ever, that age of romance,
  When heroes and saints were the boast of your song,
And your chivalric warriors still held the best lance
  For the life of the weak, and the death of the strong.

Those sires of your City, who founded her Forts,
  Her Churches and Halls, in the good olden time,
When her merchants were princes who kept open courts,
  While Bristol was yet in the joy of her prime,

They are fled to "the land of the leal," where they rest,
  In the light of their fame, for their virtues below:
There the Canynges and Colstons, and all we love best,
  With Reynolds and Whitson, in fresh laurels glow.

There Cabot, our English Columbus, is crown'd;
  And Rowley and Chatterton smile o'er their lyres;
And our Southey and Coleridge are compass'd around
  With the song, which, though ever renew'd, never tires.

There Wyrcestre stands, with his history renown'd,
  There Butler and Newton majestic repose;
With Foster, whose soul was serene as profound;
  And Hall, who transcendent in eloquence rose.

But these, like the prophet of old, have bequeath'd
  Their spirit to those who shall follow their course;
And the deeds they achiev'd, and the words which they
      breath'd,
  Shall plead in true souls with unquenchable force.

And dreams from their sleep in the tomb shall arise,
  And work in the minds of the free and the brave,
Till they, too, shall strive for eternity's prize,
  And truth's deathless oracles burst from their grave.

There are many true spirits, that yet shall be known,
In this time-hallow'd City,—on whom we rely
To give to its children a loftier tone
Of thought and of literature, never to die.

To these she must look for her future renown;
For yet they shall rally round one noble cause,
And win for old Bristol a far brighter crown,
Than e'er she has won in her conflicts and wars.

For such are the men who, in heaven's pure sight,
Have caught higher views of the still dawning age,
When pure divine Love shall arise in its might
And light the dark path of life's pilgrimage.

Then the spirit of Union shall once more illume
The cities that skulk in that darkness of hell,
Which harsh sects and parties unblushing assume,
As smugglers choose fogs, for their blundering pell-mell.

Then true, honest thinkers,—those martyrs of God,
Who now stand forsaken in silence and scorn,—
Shall speak their bold prophecies fearless abroad,
And prepare all mankind for Truth's heavenlier morn.

They shall link in one permanent, brotherly band
The best of the sons of this City of fame;
And by great men, once more, shall great actions be plann'd,
Not pitiful jobberies unworthy our name.

They shall win back Free Commerce to Bristol again;
'Free-Trade in Free-Port' our bold motto shall be;
And all men, who now of their interest complain,
Shall find their best interest in just liberty.

FRANCIS BARHAM 1847

(From)

BRISTOL BEAUTIES

Avon said to the Froome,
"Pray, sweep like a broom,
And fail not to take on me pity;
For with all your pains,
You stop up our drains,
Which serve but to poison our city!

Your numerous locks,
And your stinking docks,
Your city in want of repair;
Call loudly on Froome
To make a new broom,
Or the people will die in despair.

Now, why not be bold?
The truth must be told,
How you gave up your run to the sea;
Return'd with the tide,
A sweet scented bride,
To bring health to our ancient Quay."

Not true, master Avon,
I'm food for the salmon,
I keep a soft bed for the shipping;
And still find a bed,
That causes much dread
To sailors that must go a sipping.

Now Redcliff can boast
Of worthies a host,
If it only records a young man;
Who in youth went mad,
Its a tale too sad,
Deny this, oh, Wish if you can!

The record stood by,
On a pile most high,
A credit to one named Fripp!
But now its laid low,
No longer a show—
Young Chatterton's down in the Crypt.

Good bye to the pile,—
A pattern in style,—
And look at the Bristol Station;
In size and expense
A want of good sense,—
Quite big enough for the nation!

It's thought high treason
To ask for a reason
For making the Station so big;
As all that run in
Are certain to bring
A wish to be off with a gig.

St. Philip, good bye,
You poison the sky,
And send all your filth to the cut;
So on we must stroll
To avoid the new toll,
And visit St. Paul a new slut.

Having reached the Weir,
Frome shed a big tear,
To find all his water had flown,
Men picking his side,
Once washed by the tide,
His bottom as bare as a bone.

Look master Froome,
Is this your new broom,
That soon must be filled from the drains;
In granting my wish,
You kill all the fish,
A positive wanting of brains.

I'll stop up your drains,
And swamp your plains,
Till all my foul water is free;
I'm free as the rain,
By nature a drain,
Old Neptune I long for the sea.

Let us quit the stench,
And seek for a bench,
In our ancient College Green;
For I want repose,
For my poor old nose,
Whilst we chat with the worthy Dean.

Oh! oh! master Dean,
No bench to be seen?
No rest for the weary and old?
If its come to this pass,
Let us take to the grass,
And pray to be spared from a cold.

THE MAN IN THE SUN 1848

CLIFTON AND A LAD'S LOVE

Leigh Woods are as beautiful as when I roamed in them three years ago. The lights fall still as golden on those grey rocks streaked with red, on the ivy and the glossy trees, the ferns and heather and enchanter's nightshade. This loveliness sinks into my soul now as it did then. But it does not stir me so profoundly or painfully. I do not feel the unassuaged hunger of the soul so deeply.

The tide is high, and stormy beams
Of sunlight scud across the down:
Above, the cloudy squadrons frown;
On their broad front a rainbow gleams.

Cease, boisterous wind. The west is grey
With glory-coated mists, that swell
From distant seas, and gathering tell
Of coming storm and darkened day.

Leave the dank clouds to droop, and guide
Toward their fair port yon sleeping sails:
Close-furled they wait the wakening gales;
Shower-sprinkled shines the pennon wide.

Sail seaward, stately ship, and view
Some blessed isle where love is bred.
Bring me again my love that's dead,
And all I have I'll give to you.

The magic of divine spring sunlight is again abroad. The clearings in Leigh Woods are sheets of bluebells. The service-trees upon the cliffs have expanded their white under-leafage, with thick bosses of blossom honey-sweet; burly, big-bodied, furry bees, banded black and red, swaying helplessly, and swinging their unwieldy carcasses in air, hum drunken with honeydew and white bloom above and underneath and all around.

We clambered down the cliffs, and bruised young fennel-shoots and marjoram and thyme and the many aromatic mints and celeries that grow there. We saw the thorns in bloom, and the light upon the hanging birches of Leigh Woods, and the jackdaws glistening from shade to sunlight, as of old. Ships came up the Avon at our feet; we could almost touch the pennons waving from their masts. Then we wandered on the downs, whence we could see the channel, silvery-grey like a lake, with film behind film of Welsh hills traced upon the blue beyond. All was so calm, so clear, that the eye might trace elm-masses on the further marge of Severn, and the hedgerows of the upland fields, with here and there a patch of curling smoke.

The light from yonder cliff is fled,
That yester morn so brightly shone;
The glory of thy love hath gone
From my dulled life, and left it dead.

Let sunshine fade from rock and sky,
Let Leigh's deep woodland walks be torn;
O'er ruined woods I will not mourn,
Which once were green, when you and I

Went hand in hand among the flowers,
Whose names I taught you, and I made
Rare crowns of columbines to shade
With purple buds the golden showers

Of your loved curls. At times we hung
Like eagles o'er the dizzy rock,
Where faintly boomed the hammer's shock,
And ever upward slowly swung

The sailor's melancholy chant;
While ships went gliding out to sea,
Sails furled and pennons floating free,
With sunlight on their sterns aslant;

Till evening yellowed over all
From Hesper in the dewy sky—
The woods may fall, I will not sigh;
Love's star hath set, 'tis time they fall.

J. A. SYMONDS

DURDHAM DOWNS

This eve the Downs are red and white
  With blossoms of the may,
The chestnut trees a rich delight
  Along the asphalt way.

My steps would turn, if but they might,
  To follow my sad heart,
Where all the Downs are red and white,
  Where lovers dwell apart.

The chestnuts cast their fresh delight
  Upon the jaded eyes,
And men enraptured at the sight
  Feel Spring within them rise.

Where I have wandered many a night
  When young Love walked that way,
I know the Downs are red and white
  With blossoms of the may.

Yea, thrushes 'mid this pure delight
  Give forth the joy of Spring:
Naught there intrudes such song to blight,
  Perfect is everything.

My spirit steals in ghostly flight
  Along the winding way,
Bathes in the snowy-boughed delight
  As it were foaming spray.

This eve the Downs are red and white,
  And next spring-time, maybe,
Where chestnut trees are sweet delight,
  I shall be home to see.

WILLIAM C. POCOCK

Dublin, 1919
(Publ. in Bristol Poets' Fellowship, 1921)

CLIFTON

I'm here at Clifton, grinding at the mill
  My feet for thrice nine barren years have trod;
But there are rocks and waves at Scarlett still,
  And gorse runs riot in Glen Chass—thank God!

Alert, I seek exactitude of rule,
  I step, and square my shoulders with the squad;
But there are blueberries on old Barrule,
  And Langness has its heather still—thank God!

There is no silence here: the truculent quack,
  Insists with acrid shriek my ears to prod,
And, if I stop them, fumes; but there's no lack
  Of silence still on Carraghyn—thank God!

Pragmatic fibs surround my soul, and bate it
  With measured phrase, that asks the assenting nod;
I rise, and say the bitter thing, and hate it—
  But Wordsworth's castle's still at Peel—thank God!

O broken life! O wretched bits of being,
  Unrhythmic, patched, the even and the odd!
But Bradda still has lichens worth the seeing,
  And thunder in her caves—thank God! thank God!

FIVES'-COURT

Sometimes at night I stand within a court
    Where I have play'd by day;
And still the walls are vibrant with the sport,
  And still the air is pulsing with the sway
    Of agile limbs that now, their labours o'er,
To healthful sleep their strength resign—
But how of those who play'd with me langsyne,
    And sleep for evermore?

T. E. BROWN

Poems, 1900

BRISTOL BELLS

Sunday Evening in Spring

Soft breath of Spring, fair gleams of May upon the garden green,
Where lilac boughs are mingled with laburnum's golden sheen;
And gay with flowers along the lawn, backed by the tall elm trees,
A sweet old-fashioned border runs, the haunt of murmuring bees.
And from the ancient town hard by, in rhythmic cadence slow,
The chime of bells for Evensong, comes softly to and fro.

And down the slopes the birches hang their feathery catkin wreaths,
And yellow gorse upon the bank, a subtile fragrance breathes:
While in the border columbines, and polyanthus show
With tulips gay, and asphodel, and wallflowers all ablow.
And still from many a smoke-stained tower, borne on the light spring air,
The Bristol bells are chiming our their call to praise and prayer.

A Sunday calm seems brooding o'er the garden's shady place,
The town's dull stir of busy life is hushed a little space;
The shadows lengthen o'er the grass, the sunlight falling low
Lights up the old house on the slope, where many windows glow;
While mingled with the evening bells, in drowsy monotone,
The echo of returning rooks upon the breeze is blown.

The city and the distant hills, are bathed in evening light,
For Bristol lifts her misty veil of smoke on Sunday night,
Her spires and towers, and clustered masts of ships along the quay
Shine out beyond the fresh Spring trees, a picture fair to see.
Ah! many a tale of years gone by, that old town garden tells,
But through them all a cadence runs,—the chime of Bristol bells!

M. C. TYNDALL 1878

THE BELLS OF ABBOT'S LEIGH

In the pleasant summer gloaming,
When the birds and bees are homing,
And the sun flings gleaming diamonds round
the bosom of the sea,
When the lengthening evening shadows
Lie along the river meadows,
Then a ringing
Joy comes swinging
From the bells of Abbot's Leigh.

With the thrushes' hush-song throbbing,
Swelled to joy, or sunk to sobbing,
Borne on purring thymy breezes comes the
faery peal to me;
Even birds that hymn the mating
Pause to hear the air vibrating
With the humming
Music coming
From the bells of Abbot's Leigh.

Mine this bloomy Nature-palace,
Where the buttercup's gold chalice
Waits abrim with dewy nectar for the
festival to be;
Mine this wakened thrill of wonder
At wide skies and good earth under,
And the story
Of Heaven's glory
From the bells of Abbot's Leigh.

Here is tranquil Peace abiding,
Quiet calm in Nature hiding,
For Joy's spirit broods immortal on the
hill-tops and the sea.
Nature sings new-crowned and vernal—
"Pain is brief, but joy eternal!"
Mellow laughter
Echoes after
From the bells of Abbot's Leigh.

ROSE SHARLAND 1917

IN THE DIM CITY

(BRISTOL)

City of clanging bells
And narrow, dingy streets,
Where the continuous din of traffic swells,
The throb of commerce beats.
At times, when sundown over smoky piles
Stretches a healing hand,
There comes a touch of love that reconciles,
A glory that the soul can understand.
Round dusky roofs and spires
Eddy the driven clouds of sunset fires;
With marvellous mutation
Flames the swift mystery of transfiguration.
One moment—and we deem
Thou art the magic city of a dream;
One moment—and the gloom
Hath foiled the gleam:
City of toil, and want, and mortal doom.

Close to thine ancient walls
Come subtle whisperings of the Severn Sea.
I stand upon thy quay
Amid the noisy calls,
The dissonant cries,
The clash and hurry of thy merchandise:
And with the tide that creeps
In stained impurity,
There comes a legend of far ocean deeps,
Of cave and crag and seaward mystery.
I hear the wave that leaps
In scattered foam: the sea-birds noisily
Rifle the footprints of the ebbing tide.
One moment—and the dream hath died.
Sullied and black, the water sleeps
Forgetful of the sea-fowl's wing;
City of sordid stain, and wealth, and hungering.

A. L. SALMON 1908

THE PHOENIX-HEARTED

As from the blue, pale-flowering wave doth rise
Kuan Yin, the goddess, with her still sad eyes,
And as the phoenix flame-enraptured dies,
Yet with a fiery crest is born anew;

So China's soul lived on. In every age,
The poet pensive by the torrent, sage
Dark-browed with thought in mountain hermitage,
Where white peaks pierce the cloudy heavens through,

The patient artist striving to confine
All nature's loveliness within a line,
The maiden working with a silk so fine
Dragons of gold upon a cloth of blue.

The founder toiling through the midnight hours
To cast the sonorous bell, the subtle powers
Of potters making bowls like fragile flowers,
The emperor wise, administrator true,

The farmer, whom the furrow's narrow span
For centuries contented—through all these there ran
Old China's life-blood. And from these Japan
Learnt gentle arts, these tamed the Tartar crew.

But now across those peaceful skies
Where in the past the poet's eyes
Imagined dragons of the mist and cloud,
Stream hosts of glittering dragon-flies
To fill with dust those quiet eyes
And cover ancient beauty with a stormy shroud.

But strength in stillness lies. She is not dead.
Kuan Yin again shall raise her gracious head,
And though it fall in flames of bloody red
The phoenix shall arise with plumage proud.

IRIS MURDOCH (aged 18 years)

THE COMING OF APRIL

Spring breaks upon the land. Waves roll
Of green and gold into the gardens,
Foam white on cherry trees.
Yes, I have seen
The little puppet hands of chestnut buds
That flutter at the sun—
April's pale feet that glitter in the green,
April with bird-song came to steal my soul.

IRIS MURDOCH (aged 18 years)

STAR-FISHER

There was a young lady whose
  Chief occupation
Was fishing for stars in the
  Milky Way.
With bluebottle eyes and a
  Sense of vocation
She dangled her legs on the
  Banks of the day.

With touching affection her
  Uncles and cousins
Would come every Friday to
  Bait all her hooks,
They sat on the bank in their
  Scores and their dozens
With red velvet gaiters and
  Cookery books.

Her three elder sisters and
  Ravid relations
Were all much too haughty to
  Help with the rest,
But when she had sent them some
  Choice constellations,
On Collyfrock's Day they would
  Knit her a vest.

But the one she liked best in her
  Family Circle
Was Grandfather Gangle, with
  Garrible ears,
Down slippery skies he would
  Slide to encircle
Her wishoppy waist and half
  Drown her in tears.

And when they had had some un-
  Usually rousing
Astronomal liquor in
  Fulginous pails,
They deafened the stars with their
  Noisy carousing
And tied cauliflowers to the
  Comets' bright tails.

IRIS MURDOCH (aged 18 years)

"LOWER THAN THE ANGELS"

Out of a million years of rock
And a million years of mud,
Out of the chaos of night and day,
Out of the song the Mighty One struck
From the clanging stars in the Milky Way,
Came man in the image of God.
And how does this clear-eyed King fulfil
His glorious destiny?
He sees the earth and the blood on the earth,
Bowing his neck at a madman's call
To the yoke of servitude and death—
And the heavens he cannot see.
And did Eternity toil for this?—
Working so patiently,
Out of the lovely soulless things,
Golden lions and passionless
Fishes that glide in the green and wings
Of eagles, to fashion such frailty,
To mark God's face with the Devil's kiss?

IRIS MURDOCH (aged 18 years)

BY SEVERN'S BANKS

One voice is from the homeland and the hills,
One voice is from the grey unrestful sea.
Here where at dusk the tingling silence thrills
I linger companied with memory;
Hearing at times the boom
Of the far fog-ship sounding through the gloom;
At times the cry of nightbirds, and the sigh
Of slumberous waters nigh.

O crying from the bygone and the known—
O murmur from the hidden and mystic deep
To which we pass alone
Through paths of sleep—
I cannot hear you clear;
Earth's dust is in mine ear,
The distant voice is muffled by the near.
I stand
As on a frontierland
Of things that with a step shall be revealed,
The hitherside of regions mist-concealed;
Yet still it seems
There must be instant waking from my dreams,
When it shall be
That the unheard is heard, the unseen appear—
The message that I almost hear,
The vision that I almost see.

A. L. SALMON 1921

AS I WALKED OUT ONE EVENING

As I walked out one evening,
  Walking down Bristol Street,
The crowds upon the pavement
  Were fields of harvest wheat.

And down by the brimming river
  I heard a lover sing
Under an arch of the railway:
  'Love has no ending.

'I'll love you, dear, I'll love you
  Till China and Africa meet,
And the river jumps over the mountain
  And the salmon sing in the street,

'I'll love you till the ocean
  Is folded and hung up to dry
And the seven stars go squawking
  Like geese about the sky.

The years shall run like rabbits,
  For in my arms I hold
The Flower of the Ages,
  And the first love of the world.'

But all the clocks in the city
  Began to whirr and chime:
'O let not Time deceive you,
  You cannot conquer Time.

'In the burrows of the Nightmare
  Where Justice naked is,
Time watches from the shadow
  And coughs when you would kiss.

'In headaches and in worry
  Vaguely life leaks away,
And Time will have his fancy
  To-morrow or to-day.

'Into many a green valley
  Drifts the appalling snow;
Time breaks the threaded dances
  And the diver's brilliant bow.

'O plunge your hands in water,
  Plunge them in up to the wrist;
Stare, stare in the basin
  And wonder what you've missed.

'The glacier knocks in the cupboard,
  The desert sighs in the bed,
And the crack in the tea-cup opens
  A lane to the land of the dead.

'Where the beggars raffle the banknotes
  And the Giant is enchanting to Jack,
And the Lily-white Boy is a Roarer,
  And Jill goes down on her back.

'O look, look in the mirror,
  O look in your distress;
Life remains a blessing
  Although you cannot bless.

'O stand, stand at the window
  As the tears scald and start;
You shall love your crooked neighbour
  With your crooked heart.'

It was late, late in the evening,
  The lovers they were gone;
The clocks had ceased their chiming,
  And the deep river ran on.

W. H. AUDEN

BRISTOL AND CLIFTON

"Yes, I was only sidesman here when last
You came to Evening Communion.
But now I have retired from the bank
I have more leisure time for church finance.
We moved into a somewhat larger house
Than when you knew us in Manilla Road.
This is the window to my lady wife.
You cannot see it now, but in the day
The greens and golds are truly wonderful."

"How very sad. I do not mean about
The window, but I mean about the death
Of Mrs. Battlecock. When did she die?"

"Two years ago when we had just moved in
To Pembroke Road. I rather fear the stairs
And basement kitchen were too much for her—
Not that, of course, she did the servants' work—
But supervising servants all the day
Meant quite a lot of climbing up and down."

"How very sad. Poor Mrs. Battlecock."
" 'The glory that men do lives after them,'[1]
And so I gave this window in her name.
It's executed by a Bristol firm;
The lady artist who designed it, made
The figure of the lady on the left
Something like Mrs. Battlecock."

"How nice."
"Yes, was it not? We had
A stained glass window on the stairs at home,
In Pembroke Road. But not so good as this.

[1]Shakespeare, of course.

This window is the glory of the church
At least I think so—and the unstained oak
Looks very chaste beneath it. When I gave
The oak, that brass inscription on your right
Commemorates the fact, the Dorcas Club
Made these blue kneelers, though we do not kneel:
We leave that to the Roman Catholics."

"How very nice, indeed. How very nice."

"Seeing I have some knowledge of finance
Our kind Parochial Church Council made
Me Peoples' Warden, and I'm glad to say
That our collections are still keeping up.
The chancel has been flood-lit, and the stove
Which used to heat the church was obsolete.
So now we've had some radiators fixed
Along the walls and eastward of the aisles;
This last I thought of lest at any time
A Ritualist should be inducted here
And want to put up altars. He would find
The radiators inconvenient.
Our only ritual here is with the Plate;
I think we make it dignified enough.
I take it up myself, and afterwards,
Count the Collection on the vestry safe."

"Forgive me, aren't we talking rather loud?
I think I see a woman praying there."

"Praying? The service is all over now
And here's the verger waiting to turn out
The lights and lock the church up. She cannot
Be Loyal Church of England. Well, good-bye.
Time flies. I must be going. Come again.
There are some pleasant people living here.
I know the Inskips very well indeed."

JOHN BETJEMAN

BRISTOL

Green upon the flooded Avon shone the after-storm-wet-sky
Quick the struggling withy branches let the leaves of autumn fly
And a star shone over Bristol, wonderfully far and high.

Ringers in an oil-lit belfry—Bitton? Kelston? who shall say?—
Smoothly practising a plain course, caverned out the dying day
As their melancholy music flooded up and ebbed away.

Then all Somerset was round me and I saw the clippers ride,
High above the moonlit houses, triple-masted on the tide.
By the tall embattled church-towers of the Bristol waterside.

And an undersong to branches dripping into pools and wells
Out of multitudes of elm trees over leagues of hills and dells
Was the mathematic pattern of a plain course on the bells.*

*1	2	2	4	4	5	5	3	3	1	1
2	1	4	2	5	4	3	5	1	3	2
3	4	1	5	2	3	4	1	5	2	3
4	3	5	1	3	2	1	4	2	5	4
5	5	3	3	1	1	2	2	4	4	5

JOHN BETJEMAN

THE HOLE IN THE WALL

More a long slit
Like, and Tom,
That's where he sit
And watch out
For the Press Gang.
Tom left a hand
At the Nile see,
So they don't want 'e
Boy. When Tom gives
The "Look alive",
Then you nip
Down them stairs
Back of the bar.
Slow on the rum,
If you slip,
Like what Joe
Did, you're Jack Tar
'Fore you knows
Where you are.
Take me, never meant
For the sea.
(T'isn't the Captain
'Tis conditions, boy,
Don't know how
I come through.)
So when you
Hear Tom shout
It's down to the
Cellar, boy, and OUT.

CLAIRE HALL

NEWFOUNDLAND STREET

An old man,
in an old place
of piled stones, and griefs,
and the lame sticks, lost,
is in sand stills,
that cannot raise green days
that were song,
breaks the wills of youth on bones
from the stairs of his pain,
and loves long gone.

Old worn men grieve silently—
the long wounds of their silence
wait for no morns,
no moaning winds
sleet their consciences
or desires,
no fires, lift feet worn down—
on time's block,
the crack of dawn strikes
anew at the clock,
for each and every one
sure, and spent to one end.

This end is quiet—
stroll into the sun's fire
in the wafting wind,
a withered cheek
catching at the phrase
once sharp,
yet no voices speak,
only the voles in the ruins squeak,
the flat brass of a steel world cries,
no cry of greeting shakes
out the thin sighs,
he walks on a world of his time,
his time is sprung on surmise.

RICHARD BALL

BATHURST WHARF

The pigeons
tap the pavements
briskly,
their pouting strides
are shadowed
on the stones.

The metal stands
and chains
are at the basin's edge,
grey, gaunt iron,
surviving to balk
the leaden step
from doom.

Fleeter than foot
the gulls wheel out;

over the high, boxed stone
the cranes stoop
on their gantried hulks,
creak, to claim
the passing sense.

Only in iron
are their unhurried
axes swung,
tired iron, leaned
on its axle power.

Lower,
the shadows drift
along the quay,
the world is turning
on disparity.

RICHARD BALL

AT THE SCENE OF THE ACCIDENT—BRISTOL

Will anyone who saw the accident
Or can give any information,
Please communicate with God.

There were a few Romans with a few roads
A few monks with a Monastery
A few sailors with a few ships.

A few merchants
With an enviable reputation
For paying on the nail,
And hedging the everlasting bet
By building churches,
Outward and visible signs
Of inward and spiritual disgrace.

There was division of labour.
While St. Mary was on the Quay
St. Michael was on the Mount—Without.

Without what?
Without walls, said Cromwell,
And broke them down,
As he broke King Charles's neck.

But Bristol had the last word.
The merchants built their mansions
On the down. Whose down?
Kings Down.

And so the accident spread
Like blood and petrol on a motorway,
Coal to the East and Culture to the West.

Until Whitfield wooed Wesley to Wine Street,
And pushed him to preach at St. Philip's Marsh.
For the hearts of poor and rich—strangely warming.
Bristol, England, nor the World, his parish,
Were ever the same again. A new beginning
From a New Room. At Broadmead.

A city of many conveniences, public and otherwise.
Conveniently coloured people to trade in,
Conveniently sweet-burning weed
NICOTIANA TABACUM
To soothe the nerves of a nation
And endow monumental monstrosities.

Schools—for Chatterton to cheat at,
For Haig to happen at
For Iris Murdoch to mature at.

A bridge—for people to jump over,
A suburb for Betjeman to bumble over,
A theatre rescued from a rubbish heap.

Students and aeroplanes, both trying their wings.
Who can say which cost more?
Or which make more noise?

Accidents have inescapable attraction.
So has Bristol—for there are now
Half a million people
At the scene of the accident.

BILL PICKARD

STOKE HOUSE 1669

on Stoke Hill, Stoke Bishop
(now Trinity College)

Restoration was in the air,
Plague and fire forgotten
And the Commonwealth
Which the common folk
Scarcely saw as theirs
Was done with
And over.

The builders materials,
Straight beams
And twisted portals
And all that protects
Preserves and cossets
More fortunate mortals
Lay in clover.

Destiny shaped its ends;
Indeed, not so much
Destiny as Divinity.
From slavestop to
Salvation Station
Dedicated to the Holy
(And Undivided) Trinity.

BILL PICKARD

CLIFTON:
a lament for the Trams

Down between the dentists'
Grey rockgardens,
Red trams rattled
Down Whiteladies Road;
Yellow and scarlet the
Gay old posters,
Varnished wood carried a
Precious load,
Where C. of E.
Irvingite,
Procathedral,
Tyndale Baptist and
Redland Park,
Christchurch Clifton, and
Mount of Olives
Lurked in one warm
Religious dark.

And the Bristol Tramways Autobus Co.:
Ran down that leisurely road,
OXO advertisements flaming aglow
As they carried a precious load.

And off to the right there
Pembroke Road—
Laburna, schools and a
Nursing home—
Where All Saints' cast-copper
Steeple shewed
The Anglican path
To Rome;
Serenely behind it
Landsdowne Crescent:
Wroughtiron balconies
Bask in the sun;
From EE Salems of
1860
Westminster chimes pealed
Quarter to one.

When the Bristol Tramways Autobus Co.:
Travelling down to the Zoo,
Carried one morning three years ago
Buns for the bears and you!

Children were playing on
Clifton downs *then*
Scouting and football;
Sweaters and glee.
Down in the gorge 'neath the
Cam'ra Obscura
The sultry Avon
Crept to the sea;
But ragged the silence on
Clifton downs *now:*
Past "Bible Churchmen,"
Satchel in hand,
Children shuffle down
Granite pavements
Endless miles
Of the tired land

Since the Bristol Progress Autobus Co:
Has torn up its tramway lines,
And somewhere a dingy and elderly row
Of varnished wood slowly declines.

GERARD IRVINE

BRISTOL

How proud,
Opposed to Walton's silent towers, how proud,
With all her spires and fanes and volumed smoke,
Trailing in columns to the midday sun,
Black, or pale blue, above the cloudy haze,
And the great stir of commerce, and the noise
Of passing and repassing wains, and cars,
And sledges grating in their underpath,
And trade's deep murmur, and a street of masts
And pennants from all nations of the earth,
Streaming below the houses, piled aloft,
Hill above hill; and every road below
Gloomy with troops of coal-nymphs, seated high
On their rough pads, in dingy dust serene;—
How proudly amid sights and sounds like these,
Bristol, through all whose smoke, dark and aloof,
Stands Redcliff's solemn fane,—how proudly girt
With villages, and Clifton's airy rocks,
Bristol, the mistress of the Severn sea,—
Bristol, amid her merchant palaces,
That ancient city, sits!

W. L. BOWLES

CLERKSHIP

So it has come to digs discreet where urn
Awaits the gong that drums the famished hour.
Beyond chaste curtains, dogs in harness sour
The verges under regimental trees.

He walks the inky alleys, drain-pipe mazed
Through sparrow feud and predatory rain;
To park where children prance by lime and plane,
With gimcrack Galilee of jaded swans.

A clerkship dulls. Ledger and clock conjoin.
He window watches olden crone-toothed lanes
Keeping their cobbles under Redcliffe chime
And ships bone-searched by bowel-picking cranes.

The blood of flares his dream, when Bombers rained
Bereavements round the unavailing spire.
Fears had laid ice upon him in the cave
Of bed, till anger scalded him to war.

He killed by numbers, by remote control,
Survived all-seeing cannon, to tread
Redcliffe stone. The Channel sank her dead.
The medals tarnished in the collar drawer.

So it had come to file and ledger, warm
Under pigeon cornice. Once a year
A bugle stops the world, but Donne's bass bell
Tolls over stamping Europe. Fear

Climbs him again like bindweed. Shall he lie
Ninepin length, no pennies for the eyes?
Chancel and nave succumb? Houses kneel?
No tally to the number of his days?

Cornice and curtain hide in mousy shade
His aspen limbs. He prays himself unseen
For slaughter;—when next the bombers run
Their long deaths over Evensong.

SEA WALLS, OCTOBER 1944

Rust corroded, cruel fanged, the wire writhes, an evil hedge
Across the road to the Downs.
And where the prams and cars and couples thronged
In the distant days of peace,
Massive and cold the Nissen sheds
Sprawl, black whales astride the grass.
The dead leaves fall on the brooding
Machines that wait in serried rows their call.
Ducks, tanks, amphibians—all the devilry
Of a knacker's yard is theirs, designed
To tear the sinews of the waiting cattle.
One moves with terrifying snarl and sudden
Flaying of earth under tracks. A khaki girl
red-nailed, turreted, paints her lips
Unheeding the steel's grim work.
The tank moves on, its shuddering strength
Still beats the air as the engine's note withdraws
And overhead the daws wheel to land . . .

In the grey October light
The Sea Walls, derelict, forbidden,
Wait for the lads to walk their paths again.
Across the gorge the dark inhibitive green of the firs
Masses secret and sullen amid the autumn tints.
No sound or sign of the city below
Only the gulls and the tanks and away
To the west the smoke of Avonmouth and the Denny's hump
Mingle in the unreal light.
There's a shiver of wind, the leaves fall
Melancholy, unceasingly,
And over the Downs a sigh . . . and a waiting
For the day when these alien shapes are gone
Never to return in a world of sanity.

NICHOLAS H. LANGRAN

BALLAD OF THE FIVE CONTINENTS

In blue Bristol city at tall-tide I wandered
  Down where the sea-masts their signals were shining,
  I heard a proud seaman on the poop-deck reclining
Shout to the stars that about the ship blundered
  On the high harbour lie six shifty daughters
  Their bodies are straight, their eyes are wide
  Here is the key of their burly bedchamber
I have unlocked it, I replied.

As I went down Water Street beneath the blond sun
  The trees of cold Christmas screaming with starlings
  Sweet screamed the birds as my delicate darlings
Scanned at my hand the black-buttered gun
  Think of the collar my bonny, my beauty
  Think of the hangman with hands so red
  Pray, pray that he does his duty
I am that hangman, I said.

As I walked in Wine Street the silk snow was falling
  And night in her Asian hair hung her comb,
  Soft sang the yellow-faced seaman of home
The gong and the coconut-fiddle recalling
  In the vermilion forest the dancer
  Adorns with gold thorns his holy head
  Will you not seize his hands, his fingers?
I am the dance, I said.

In Bread Street in summer we saw the boys hauling
  The Yankee-white wheat on the bowl of the bay,
  Between us the sword of the sun where we lay
Bloody with poppies, the warm sky our shawling
  Sly sing the sirens on the coast of California
  The oyster-fingered, the easy-eyed,
  Tiding their tune in the gin-wicked palaces
The song is mine, I cried.

Down by the dockside the green ships groaning
  Ten-roped writhe on the ragged sea,
  Blessed are they with the laurel tree
Now in the prow stands a saint for the stoning
  Sound the salt bell on the mound of the ocean
  Fish for a prayer in the pool of the dead
  When the storm strikes, speak the word on the waters
I am that word, I said.

ENVOI

I am the Prince
I am the lowly
I am the damned
I am the holy.
My hands are ten knives.
I am the dove
Whose wings are murder.
My name is love.

CHARLES CAUSLEY

CRISTO DE BRISTOL

The 'Cristo de Bristol' is an articulated figure of Christ used for the Easter Sepulchre and carried through the streets of a fishing village of northern Spain during the Holy Week processions. It is said to have been dredged from the Avon by a Spanish sea-captain, who brought the figure to his home port.

I am the Bristol Christ,
That waking man who won
With hands of wire the Easter fire
Out of the Biscay sun.
Cast in my coat of lights
Upon the poking tide
A seaman with a snare of stars
Hauled me to his side.

Swim on, Captain Jesus,
Wherever you may wish.
Write on the wicked water
The message of the fish.
Heal in the holy river
Your five and fingered scars,
Turn like a tree about the sea
Your skeleton of spars.

I stepped from off the ocean
Upon the sea-struck shore,
I laid me down my cruel-crown
Before my father's door.
I carried him that kingdom
I set beneath my skin
That he might seal the sorrow
Of all the world within.

Now springs upon your shipmast
The burning bush of day,
From your shot side the breathing tide
Wears the black grave away.
Bless with your fan of fingers
These hands, this heart, these eyes,
And lift my love and fishes
Perfect, to paradise.

CHARLES CAUSLEY

TEMPLE CHURCH

"This monument is not open to the public",
this was indicated on a wooden sign
that had been nailed outside the door,
the reason, partly
was that this building
was roofless over a barren floor;
more, the tower leaned
and the houses around
caricaturised the flaw;
a pigeon alighted on the ridge of a wall
and I wondered whether its weight
would make the whole edifice fall.

The stonework was edged with trimmed mortar
that had been masoned almost timelessly hard;
nearby there were the carved tombstones
that referred undecipherably to people's beloved,
these slabs had been shifted to the cemetery edge
to make place for a lawn over the place of the dead
and there were benches on the sides of the pathways
a place of rest for the strangers passing by.

I remained here by the skeletonised church's side
which seemed surplus to the parochial need
and I wondered
what Jesus thought,
and was he the unemployable kind,
and would he say that really
with what had happened, that he did not mind?

ABE ADAMS

WITHIN THE CITY LIMITS

"The fairest, goodliest and most famous parish church
in England" rocks against the ruffian cars
that vie beneath its spire. In the port
an alien ship can blow a storm.

Within its sight I went to school.
I suffered at my seniors' hands,
only to nail my retributions
on softer heads than mine.

And Nayler, the Quaker, suffered here.
He thought himself a Christ,
and rode through Bristol in the rain
as if he viewed it as a new Jerusalem.

Rain or no rain,
the Lord Protector's vigilantes saw quite clearly.
Unease needs scapegoats;
no better scapegoat than this "horrid blasphemy".

"The tongue that bored through Christ"
itself was bored, the body slashed, branded,
and parcelled back
within the shadow of this church.

Nayler rode again,
but this time arse to nose,
bared to the beadle's cat,
Buttocks are always good for a laugh.

The tracery has just been cleaned.
Radiant now, it dims 'YOU DIRTY WOGS'
scrawled on a nearby wall, and outshines
even the neon screen that spits out news of napalm.

ALAN CRANG

VOYAGE 47

The present dies—like music—in the moment of creation,
Through its narrow door the future slips away
Into the unreturning past, the nearest and the furthest instants
Equally remote and irretrievable. The years that make us older
Spirit everything away; sand castles crumbling in the tides
Of long ago; a century whose mighty fleets
Have sailed away for ever. Someone else's world
Becomes involved in the machinery of Time
With its iron slowly rusting
Like the gentle death of Autumn.

But though the epochs glide away like drifting leaves.
Upon the wake of History we see
The shining beauty of the journey
Up to now. Far across the surface
Of that secular and distant sea,
Multitudes of predecessors stumbled
Like reiterating waves. Yet certain rarer spirits rose
As if from stereoscopic depths, their passion for perfection
Manifested on the tablets of the mind, becoming
Legendary pages in the book of the immense departed.

Out of the shadowy mist then let us beckon forth—
Isambard Brunel—one of those who made the morning,
Iron master, little giant, poet-engineer,
Whose every faculty was fused in the creative centre,
Mind, machine and principle transmuted by his native fire.
In every generation the original goes out to use the world
And taste the hours of life at its most living;
Unexampled, absolute beginners
Reaching out beyond their curiosity,
Belonging to another age before it has existed.

So he was born to dream awake a visionary future.
In a sunburst of ideas, the pencil whispering to the paper,
Came the manuscript design of his most daring vessel;
No mere shuffling paddler, no slow, processional sailing swan,
But an invincible leviathan to match the sea's gigantic moods.
With quietly exalted strength,
This prophet of the holy power of size
Inscribed his testament, preparing our arrival
At the country of tomorrow, setting out
To float an iron mansion on Victorian waters.

In that long, long nineteenth century of our imagination,
Life was slow and deep and things had time
To be significant. But was their world so unperplexed,
Who built the first of the global liners,
Laying the keel of a long tradition?
I see the father brooding over the difficult birth,
Until at last his giant brain-child wakened
To disturb a city's majesty. Then with what genial amplitude
The happy bands blared forth in brass explosion
Under the rapturous flags as she was launched—

S.S. Great Britain—now this name begins in time to show
The pageant of her memories as if by some
Interior magic lantern. First we see her,
Fresh from the initiate fires, asleep upon the water's lap,
A canopy of seagulls slowly orbiting her cradle of nativity
Like cupids. Then the god within the furnace speaks,
In whispers of Promethean power releasing ancient sunlight
Under the sizzling boilers into the beauty of ponderous engines
Sighing with steam in their iron throats. And now
She gently leaves the standing mirror with a smile of ripples.

Soon she reappears in the Atlantic's long, grey, windswept acres,
Hull down in a waste of waters, lifted on horizons
By a thread of smoke; sliding south to purple summer seas,
To the silent rains of moonlight, the funnel trailing sparks
Like a bearded comet streaming in the firmament;
A model for the world to copy, lonely in that dawn
Of metal vessels till companioned by successors,
By the tall, dramatic steamers and the grand, white yachts
Of empire on a planet growing full of situations,
All its ocean gleaming bright and brave with shipping.

Great Britain, now a veteran, embarks on voyage 47,
Only to be battered in a roaring seascape,
Limping to a distant port, abandoned by advancing years.
Life goes on in music halls, in gaslight and the groaning trams.
Dolls all over England go in mourning for a dignified old lady
Wearing diamonds in her bonnet. Clocks go ticking on into
Another century. Great wars arrive to drink the blood of nations.
In Falkland's isles the iron castles come and go
Like thunder in a hill of clouds. And now the proud inventions
Of our bristling afternoon prepare the ruins of the future.

But in every generation there are some who look for roots;
The changeless past, for them, is a perpetual presence.
History, they know, is where we come from. So in history
They sought S.S. Great Britain—and discovered she was still alive,
Though only just. She stood upon her tottering reflection
Like a drab ghost of her former self, dying the death of furniture,
Cracks across her iron hull zigzagging like black lightning
In a sky of grey. Skilfully they laboured to repair her,
With their metal's newborn strength they patched up yesterday
And brought her safely home into the haven of eternal fame.

Now high and dry above her ancient ways, gradually
Forgetting water, silent as a dream she stands, a stranded ark
Transmitting our humanity. As after storms light rainbows down,
So does the towering spirit shine of those no longer in the world,
The lively dead. Thus from her deck I see again the bible gaze
Of all her captains sailing over a sea of creatures,
Transversing the ages as though nothing lay between and all
The outspread years were drawn together; for who can tell—perhaps
In some foreverness all that has existed still exists and we may be—
Like this great ship—harbouring a secret immortality.

ROBERT GORDON

THE BRISTOL UNICORNS

Chamber of Commerce and Committee
   Coughed in their collective beard
When to the white and ship-shape city
   Two gold unicorns appeared,

Baleful in their lorry cradles,
   Snorting for a virgin love
Above the cranes and asphalt ladles,
   What could they be thinking of

Appearing, such incongruous symbols
   Sporting horns on College Green
Just as we had sent to limbo
   Our million-petticoated Queen.

MAURICE CARPENTER

SONG TO A MYTHICAL BEAST

unicorn, unicorn,
How much strontium is borne
to melt the valour of your horn?

You should know before the rest
where the danger, whose the test.

Down below you in the street
suspect dust invades our feet.

Round about us in the town
poisoned rain comes softly down.

unicorn, unicorn,
On the red wings of the morn
what genetic twist is borne?

Grasses rich from sun and flood
menace the wisdom of our blood.

Each cloud mushroomed into space
points a warning to the race.

Nailed with power wrenched from the sun
all may be destroyed by one.

unicorn, unicorn,
Bright dawns rise where hope is born,
the crust of night is hourly torn.

Outside time the rockets fly,
man must measure, man must try.

Millions cry the end of this
corruption of the godhead's kiss.

Blast us with your mighty horn,
man is waiting to be born.

NORMAN HARVEY

EARLY DAYS

I came to Bristol in the month of May
And by July felt still a stranger here.
In the warm evening of one summer day
I walked up Clifton Down, and thought I saw
A great dark bird that hovered in the sky,
Dipping and circling, fluttered by updraughts,
Watchful and ominous, so real that I
Could not believe it just a paper kite
Until, by the Observatory tower,
I saw a young man hold its tugging string,
Balancing his weight against its power.
He wore a double necklace made of teeth
Over singlet and trousers of pure white—
Yes, long and ancient teeth, whether of giants
Or animals I do not know.
                                        A flight
Of insects I had never seen before
With brown hard coverings over their wings,
Came swarming everywhere; the young man's friends
Ran screaming, laughing, from the harmless things,
Which only tickled underneath their shirts,
But he remained aloof, communing still
With his dark flier high above the ground.
Then a large baleful woman climbed the hill,
Loomed in pale blue against the sunset sky,
And called an earnest warning to us all
That there was danger from a poisoned bird
Which was about to make the tower fall
And the cliff crumble underneath our feet.
People should keep away from it, she cried,
And hurried off, declaiming to her dog.
Did all this have some meaning? Mystified
By insects, teeth and prophecies of doom,
I thought, bemused in the uncanny light:
"What a strange place I've come to!"
                                                        But perhaps
It was the same everywhere else that night?

FREDA BROMHEAD

CLIFTON MORNING

Up here in Clifton mist blots out the Gorge,
The sunlit Bridge makes a white stitch in space.
Street pavements must be shared by shaggy youth
And permed or balding heads, but neither side
Admits encounter—glances simply slide
Over each other.

Houses here persuade
That there was once a wise and tranquil age:
Sane windows, kind verandahs, noble doors,
(Six or eight-panelled, ornamented with
Brass sphinx or an authoritative fist
Grasping a baton and a laurel wreath.)
Listen—a wedding's high euphoria!
Pink lavatory paper in festoons
About the bridal car, slogans inscribed
In shaving cream: "It's legal!!" "Instant sex!"
"Sex now!"

But let us climb the lookout tower
On Clifton Down and, like the gods, observe
The images of people unaware
That to amuse us they are thrown upon
The Camera Obscura's viewing-table.
We can watch scolding parents, loving lovers,
Trotting dogs—mists dispersing, woods descending,
The grey tide rising in the river, grass
Stretching for miles, and weather coming up
Out of the estuary; change perhaps
Impending, too. Oh yes, this is the way
The world goes, on an ordinary day.

FREDA BROMHEAD

BRISTOL—CITY OF SADNESS

Or so it was described to me
By writer friends Just visiting—
And I agree.
The sadness of the has-been
The sadness of the man who sells his soul
For a quick buck
A fast car
And through routes for all salesmen
In white Cortinas
The sadness of the empire builder
Who builds and builds
Obsessively relentlessy remorselessly
Without feeling
Save that the tower blocks and offices
Should dwarf all previous edifices.
From my office window
I look down on to a church spire
And watch day by day
Its transformation into a quaint toy
Tolerated as a token
Of what's been swept away
Into the oblivion of 'progress'.

MARIAN LIEBMANN

DOUBLE YELLOWS

Tower Lane.
Damp musty smell of old walls
High above me
The cobbles are so rough
They hurt my feet.
Narrower and narrower—
How is it that it's still
A two-way street?
The double yellow lines on both sides
Seem laughably unnecessary . . .
I turn a corner and
The dank walls
Crowd in on me
What's more, the double yellow lines
Meet in the middle of the road!

MARIAN LIEBMANN

CITY SKIN

The new skins tremble on the rails
waiting to be bought, to be brought
to life. Hot shop fans shiver them:
wraiths who beg to dance: shadows
aching for bodies—
o try mine! try mine!

I am not the gingham skin crisp
and inexperienced. Nor the black
silk that clinging hopefully
to erotic zones denies all else.
The muslin skin won't have me
insisting on a cool and placid
corpse to cover and none
of these personalised skins
defines me.

The skin of The Downs
that lie beyond the town
tempt me with their green billows.
The trees there, cascading their silks,
would take me: their knowing arms
would enfold me—if I could come.

I cannot come today.
On my way in the city
the surprised faces of sad women
and of idling, homeless men
called, "O try mine! Try mine!"
and now no other skin but theirs
will fit.

DIANA HENDRY

CLIFTON

Clifton, in vain thy varied scenes invite—
The mossy bank, dim glade, and dizzy height;
The sheep that starting from the tufted thyme,
Untune the distant churches' mellow chime.

W. S. LANDOR *An English Scene*

SLUM CLEARANCE

One morning at the back of Centre, below Park Row
(From "Bristol 63: impressions in three aspects")

The gull dive, heart in mouthing
Tension of a cycle sweeping
Toward a corner back—tingles.
The tense wait for the ripping
Sound of Styx-steel on road . . . . .
And then the disappointed relief
Of disaster averted as the steel-shanked
Gull pulls rich in love
From its head-long drop.

Your heart climbs down rich with passion
Lashed to a fury by a muttering tongue.

The wall is down and
Rubble blocks our way.
The path is deep
In broken stones.
As a steel ball swings
The shadows flee like
Hedge-hid rats rustling
Through the leaves.
We turn and go another way.
The steps steep-climb
Past ghosts of walls
Red blushing in their nakedness,
Stripped by the swinging ball.

Memories of past excitement,
Of lawlessness, of climbing
Up the rotten stairs
Of sarcophagi houses,
Of kicking open a nailed-up door
And entering in, to the dust,
The bag of nails, and the
Volume of a history book,
The fleas dancing out of the cracks
Between the ghost-paced planks.

The hole in the ground where
We went to smoke, which
Smelt of piss and dust;
The joy of fear
As a lusty man
Chased us down a road.

The dark beloved shadow,
Memories filled with Egyptian
Image of lank dark hair
And of rounded breasts . . . of
A rumpled cardigan, the
Ripples giving the breast beneath
A strange and abstract form;
The memories of another
Love, of a zip unzipped
And the soft cat-fur feel
Of a naked back, soft
As a breeze unfelt, just
Heard by the tinkling bells.

But the wall is down
And only ghosts strut
Now in our loved
Ghost town.

All is gone, dust
And smoke and pyre;
The sun soft paints
The dying walls waiting
For the hammer's blow;
Men work, tearing down
The blinds of green
Mourning weeds from trees
To pile them on the pyre.

The ghost-rich air
Is scrubbed and washed
Behind the ears by
A mother-armed sun:
The sunbeams, the moving muscle
Forearm rhythm of her work.

M. C. BEECHING (Bristol Grammar School)

A ROMAN TOMBSTONE

found at Sea Mills, and now in Bristol Museum

Above, a girl's head, crudely carved.
Below, inscribed in red,
The hope of Gaius Sentius.

Soldier, businessman or bureaucrat,
Sentius doubtless dulled his gnawing ache
With the daily opiate of duty
And took it half forgotten to his grave.
Yet after sixteen hundred years
Our own mortality still gives
A Roman's broken hopes the power to hurt us.

C. H. HOBDAY

CHATTERTON

In the city that gave away
The High Cross to adorn a banker's garden
He built himself another city
Out of mysterious sonorous words
Culled from glossaries and pocketed
As a boy hoards glittering pebbles.
He peopled it with resurrected dead
And Canynge with his monkish merchant's face
Rose from his tomb, extending
His alabaster hands in benediction.
But a gale of cruel laughter
Scattered the shining city
And blew the ghosts to air
And in the cold dark attic
With tears of rage and spited pride
A tired child has sobbed himself asleep.

C. H. HOBDAY

ORDER

Look down upon the city,
A thousand purring cars converge
And thousands more pour in
And human freight by bus and train,
Commute as ants to build their hills.
Their hills of merchandise and forms
Their hills of sales and deals.
Of contracts, orders, purchases,
Revolving of the wheels
That whirr and whirr, and grind and grind
Till rushing, bustling, mad mankind,
Is sapped of all his outward calm,
Of all his inward graces.
Look into eyes that dart with fear,
Confusion covered faces.
Look down with pity.

Look down upon the city,
A thousand purring cars have gone
And thousands more are still.

The human freight by bus and train
Commuting back to homes again
Have left their merchandise and forms
Have ceased their sales and deals
Have purchased, ordered, all their needs,
Have satiated all their greeds.
The whirring wheels have come to rest
And all the world has swiftly flowed
Like ebbing tide on rippling sand
Till all confusion's voices cease
And order reigns and night and peace.
Yet still with pity
Look down upon the city.

JOHN CLEE

SUMMER IN CLIFTON

As in a contemplative mood
I stood on the Suspension Bridge
Feeling that everything was good
My neck was bitten by a midge.
The very great—the very small—
How wonderful they are. That's all.

DONALD HUGHES

BRISTOL FASHION

Brig-stow the bridge-place
(between ocean, space?)
spanning enigma of caution
in adventurous face;

equating Vincent, Goram,
giants hewing a gorge,
with cash on the nail, slave dealing,
evangelical zeal;

where lie in catalytic eyes
Canynges' fervour, Cabot twinkling on,
an iron glint of Brunel,
a Chattertonian tear;

where coldly blue as Bristol glass
seem the lads before light gleams through,
Where the smooth-skinned, golden lasses
are sweet-kissed as Bristol Cream;

where queenly Clifton arches her back
and stretches for a crown of Downs,
where Blackboy bows to Whiteladies
while Filton tunes the Mach X sounds.

Seasplash, skyflash
in the stolid spirit of Bristol fashion
for those who would slow
to feel a city's glow.

ROBIN LLOYD

GENIUS AHOY!

(Brunel's Great Britain returns home)

Aboard a barge a rusted hulk rides home
through tides of history that lap past shores
of all horizons in a world furled in
when Bristol fashion iron first cut foam
and merchants ventured safer in the wake
than admirals who sailed with hearts of oak.
The tides and time it seems at last must pause
upon a hulk being towed the final mile
(of linear, not latitudinal scale)
—the vision of a symbol as it looms
beneath a metal rainbow that is hurled
more than a century across a gorge;
suspended in our head his dreams that forged
the bridge, the ship—together for a while.
His tides that lap all nations pound the blood
as iron rides the concept and its flood.

ROBIN LLOYD

THE DUTCH HOUSE

destroyed by enemy action 24th November 1940

Dipped lights move unsteadily through darkness
As fog clings around dampened streets.
Timbers fray with moonbeams
Into shutter drawn silence,
Crumbling from the shielded walls.

Skies ablaze in blooded tumult
Discharge spurted momentary shells
Pulsating beneath fallen metal shafts,
As paired plastered eyes
Blink from thoughts of conscious
Broken limbs nailed and buried
With bombers drifting into night fire.

ANDREA HOPKINS

THE OLD GRAVEYARD, CLIFTON

Untouched as yet by ring road planners;
A sanctuary where seasons pass
Over the crumbled years,
And curving carved calligraphy of family names,
Crossed and scrolled;
Where Anne Green lies in her maiden bed
Of sepulchred simplicity.

A caged green walk;
Wrought iron reaching,
Where pleached limes flick the tunnel lamplight
On flagstones, wet and snail slime scribbled.

A garden, sub-tropical, moss trodden,
Shrouded in folds of shrubbery and flowering grass;
Cedared and ring doved, rooked and squirrelled,
Pungent in fox foot mornings,
Whispered in noons of high-rise poplars.

A poodled pasture,
Corporation kept and clipped,
Cat-prowl walled,
Strutted with student night-time laughter.

A surburban oasis,
A remainder,
A leaning place for time,
Where quiet Anne Green in everlasting maidenhood
Lies forgotten,
But for the noting of her graven name.

JILL RACY

THE DOWNS

Across the grass where sea winds sweep and grieve,
Walking late in summer I found peace.
Under pale transparencies of leaves,
Gently, slowly, came release.
Life glittered, tantalised and then withdrew
Its offers, which had seemed so much,
And by withdrawing to some monster grew,
A giant swollen from too small a touch.
Half begun, the kiss that was unkissed;
The hand a moment's contact left alone;
Hair strands blown and fallen soon away;
Unmeant promises to tempters grown
Made me clumsy, cruel and ill at ease.
But walking late with you, I found my peace.

JILL RACY

AN EARLY PARACHUTE DESCENT IN BRISTOL

Once in Victoria's golden age,
When crinolines were all the rage,
A dame in fashionable attire
Would change life here for one up higher.
So up to Clifton Bridge she went,
And made a parachute descent.
But though 'twas not the lady's wish,
A boatman hooked her like a fish,
And thus a slave to fashion's laws
Was snatched from out death's hungry jaws.
This story's true I'd have you know,
And thus it only goes to show—

WILLIAM E. HEASELL

There was a young fellow named Sistall,
Who shot three old maids with a pistol.
When 'twas known what he'd done,
He was given a gun
By the unmarried curates of Bristol.

BRISTOL THEMES

Heroic graffiti
on treacherous rockface.
And upriver
regal Victorian bridge coolly
admonishing the brutishness
of the Portway.

Subtle cajolery at the Basin
   ships make their entrances and exits
      without appearing to move.

August cathedral   facing
crescent of secular power
   incredible mass of tiny bricks
embracing a lawn
          in this city that grows
   by X number of commercial floors
       X square-yards of concrete

weekly unprecedented snarl-ups.

You're not a city called Miracle.

But thank you anyway
for those officers of high reflection
who stand in for the lights at
      over-wrought junctions

thanks
          for
              the esoteric sidestreets
still undiscovered
              by commuters—

for the temporary abatement
      of down-to-earth voices
that rally the ratepayers
      against modern art
because its meaning   like life's
      is obscure

      thanks thanks
for the quaint and marvellous things
      we take for granted
in this city
never called Write-Off.

RAY WEBBER

REFLECTIONS OF BRISTOL

I Remember, I remember the house
where I was born.
A post-war babe, in a side-street,
nursing off Bristol's breast,
And the sun rose and the moon set.
Surely more beautifully than anywhere else.

Bristol, where I acted out my childhood fairytale.
I caught my first fish in Eastville Lake,
and tho' it was only a tiddler in a glass jar
it seemed as big as a salmon to me then.
I ran amok the bomb sites and
blazed my indian trail along Bristol's
dusty side-walks, near Stapleton Road,
squeezing thro' the station bars
unseen, to catch train numbers.
The conkers we collected near the Gorge,
then watching as the tiny toy-cars
sped from our giddy gaze 'neath
the Suspension Bridge.

Bristol of my youth, of the coffee-bars
and dance floors, and of my first love.
The summer strolls upon the Downs,
and the wet afternoons spent in the City Museum.

Bristol of my working day,
as I join the grumbling crowds
jostling bus-wards at days end.

Reflections of the years,
crystallised in flesh,
breathing life from stone.
The tourist seeks the soul of Bristol,
Frantically searching its stones and churches,
as it passes him by every second,
pulsating in its native children's breasts.
For are we not simply a reflection of
All that we love.

ELIZABETH MAGGS

BRISTOL

An Exile's View

Returning
as to some aged mother,
changed
but not destroyed
still her rich heart
fed
by river arteries,
sends
her fingers
stretching seaward,

though she's old
and multistoried scars
diminish
but can't hide
her slender elegance
and if her industries
have lined her
still her wrinkles
are endured
with dignity

but
sprightly too
confounds her critics
still expands
and throbs with life
always seeking new horizons
even in the stars
she spreads
her strong yet gentle
influence.

DAVE SAMPSON